HOW TO
JESUS W
OF EMBARRASSMENT

HAVE I GOT NEWS FOR YOU!

DUFFY ROBBINS

ZondervanPublishingHouse
Grand Rapids, Michigan

A Division of HarperCollins*Publishers*

Have I Got News for You!

Requests for information should be addressed to:
Zondervan Publishing House
Grand Rapids, Michigan 49530

Robbins, Duffy.
Have I got news for you! : how to talk about Jesus without dying of embarrassment / Duffy Robbins.
p. cm.
Originally published: Nashville, Tenn. : Graded Press, 1988.
ISBN 0-310-37461-8 (paper)
1. Witness bearing (Christianity)—Juvenile literature. 2. Teenagers—Religious life. [1. Witness bearing (Christianity) 2. Christian life.]
I. Title.
BV4520.R582 1993
248'.5—dc20 93-2114
CIP
AC

Edited by J. Cheri McLaughlin
Cover and interior design by Jeff Sharpton
Cover illustration by Von Glitchka

Printed in the United States of America

93 94 95 96 97 /❖DH/ 10 9 8 7 6 5 4 3 2 1

TABLE OF CONTENTS

BEAUTIFUL FEET

CHAPTER 1

This chapter is about feet. I admit it. The topic of feet doesn't exactly start the adrenaline flowing. When most of us think of feet, we imagine odors, itches, warts, and good luck (unless, of course, you're a rabbit). The Bible, however, talks about feet as works of art, masterpieces, a wonder to bring tears to the eyes. (My gym shoes made my eyes water once. Does that count?)

In the Old Testament we read these words:

> How beautiful on the mountains are the feet of those who bring good news, who proclaim peace, who bring good tidings, who proclaim salvation, who say to Zion, "Your God reigns." (Isaiah 52:7)

Like most people, you may be asking yourself, *Why get so excited about a pair of feet? What's the big deal?*

Actually, those feet represent a messenger on the move, somebody bringing good news from the top. When you're in a bad situation, somebody bringing good news is a beautiful sight.

One time when I was a little boy I was trapped in the crawl space under our house. The crawl space was dark, scary, wet, and lonely. Plus, at four years old, I was absolutely convinced that a monster lived down there. I'm still not sure how the crawl space entranceway got jammed. But I vividly recall staring out of the little grill, my eyes scanning the small space of outside light that I could see.

After about half an hour down there, a meter reader came by our house to do his thing. First, I heard footsteps. Then, looking through my little grill, I saw two dirty work boots moving in the direction of my screams. That was the moment I learned that feet can be beautiful. Because I knew those dirty work boots represented good news—release and no more monster!—they looked beautiful.

The word Isaiah uses to proclaim his message of peace and promise is *salvation*. Now, for most of us, that word *salvation* conjures up images of uniformed people standing around kettles at Christmastime ringing bells. But in reality, the word just means "saved." Instead of saying that a little boy was scared spitless, stuck in the crawlspace with nothing to do but worry and wait until he was found by a meter man who unjammed the door, we might just say, "The boy was saved by a meter man," or "The meter man gave the boy his salvation."

YOU, TOO, CAN HAVE BEAUTIFUL FEET!

The world we live in isn't much different from the world to which Isaiah brought his good news of peace and promise. Like the world at the time of ancient Israel, ours is a world in which nations war with one another, political jealousies threaten world peace, and people are left homeless because of centuries-old hostilities.

In many ways we are people trapped in personal and private crawl spaces, where darkness constantly threatens to close us in, and where loneliness is an everyday fact of life. Probably sitting next to you in school are people who can't even spell Isaiah and who never thought of a foot as being beautiful. But in some ways they are just as broken and hopeless as the people of Israel centuries ago.

In the midst of all the fear and hurt, God sends us forth to announce again the great news that God is in control and that he has provided an incredible plan of release and promise for all people. Our call, if we consider ourselves followers of Jesus Christ, is to move out on beautiful feet (that requires getting off our beautiful seat!) and announce to the captives that God still has a plan.

GOD HAS A PLAN

God's plan has been unfolding from the beginning of time, but a lot of folks still aren't completely clear about what the plan means. Take me, for instance. When I was a teenager I was clueless about Christianity. I didn't know anything about God or the Bible. I was so ignorant of the good news that I thought John 3:16 referred to a bathroom on the third floor. That's too bad—we can't announce the good news if we don't understand what it is.

To get excited about announcing God's good news, we have to understand that God's plan is real. God's Word is truth. Yet most of us see the Ten Commandments as Ten Suggestions or Ten Neat Ideas or Ten Options If You're Religiously Inclined. We don't seem to catch on that God's laws are as certain as the laws of nature.

BREAKING THE LAW OF GRAVITY

I've never met a sane person who didn't take seriously the law of gravity. If people see someone about to fall off a ladder, they warn that person immediately. They don't stroll up to the person and shyly ask, "Pardon me, do you believe in the law of gravity?"

We all believe in the law of gravity. We all sense the foolishness of ignoring the law of gravity. Everyday around us we see reminders that this law of gravity is for real. That's why no one ever walks up to you in the school parking lot and whispers, "Hey, psst. Friday night, you and me. Let's go out and break the law of gravity!"

What about the person who jumps off a building, you may ask. Isn't he or she breaking the law of gravity? Not really. It's more like the law of gravity is going to break them. Even if you psyched yourself into thinking, *I'll be the one who beats the law of gravity*, within seconds of taking the leap, you would experience the classic rude awakening and discover that you were wrong. Messy wrong.

What happens, though, is that we don't usually see that kind of immediate and final evidence that God's laws are real. So a lot of people remain unconvinced that God's plan is anything to be taken seriously. We regularly see people breaking God's laws, but we seldom see them suffer any consequences. It's as if God's plan isn't really a law at all—just an option if you want to believe it.

In truth, God's laws are every bit as real as nature's laws—and breaking them brings every bit as much pain and tragedy. It's just that when God's laws are broken, the crash doesn't always come immediately. Sometimes the pain comes weeks, months, or even years later. But the pain always comes.

That's why God authored his plan from the beginning. God knows best how life is to be lived. A lot of us picture God as some kind of cosmic Scrooge who made up all these commandments just to keep humans unhappy. The common notion is that if something is fun, then God is probably against it!

That crazy idea hangs on because we all know Christians who are anything but joyful and full of life. And when you're a teenager, you always seem to hear people talk about God and his plan in very grim terms. When I was in ninth grade, I had a Sunday school teacher whose basic approach to sex was, "Sex is dirty, so save it for the one you love." Her explanation didn't sound like good news to me.

No thanks to her, I now understand that God lays down certain boundaries for sexual behavior, not because sex is dirty but because experiencing sex in a way that violates God's guidelines eventually causes a lot of pain.

Those of us with beautiful feet can't wait around to see if people believe God's plan is true or not—and if they do, then tell them of God's promises. If we really believe that God has a plan and that God's plan offers peace and good news, we've got to get busy taking that message to our friends. We can't just take a *stand* for Jesus; we need to take a *walk* for Jesus!

HUMANS HAVE A PROBLEM

But there's more. You see, to help people really understand God's plan, we've got to do more than just announce the good news. We've got to be willing to also share the bad news. After all, for us to appreciate the good news of being saved, we need to understand the bad news of being lost. Having peas for dinner may not seem like good news, for example, until you find out that the only other alternative is okra. All of a sudden, you're kind of thinking, "Bring on the peas!"

The Bible teaches that God has a plan—that's good news. But the Scripture also teaches that humans have their own plan—that's bad news. Following the human plan is a problem. This problem is what Scripture describes as sin. The bad news about sin is an important part of the announcement of good news: God has a plan; we have a problem.

Though most of us have heard of sin, few of us take sin seriously these days. But God does!

One day when I was about seven years old, my brother and I found out that a girl who lived down the street from us was in her backyard sunbathing in a bikini. Now, of course, we didn't mean to do anything bad. We were just hiding behind the cars in her driveway, playing with our binoculars. But as my brother jockeyed for a better focus, he slowly backed into a big glass milk jug sitting on the porch. The next sound we heard was a huge crash as this jug fell off the porch and shattered on the driveway. At this point, Shelley, the backyard angel, jumped up from her towel and just started cursing us like crazy—calling us every name in the book and a few names that weren't even in our book. At seven years old I didn't know enough of what the words meant to be offended, but I could tell she was very angry.

Well, we took off running for home. We were scared to death. I had never been chased by a seventeen-year-old girl in a bikini, and somehow this didn't seem like one of those "Mr. Rogers' Moments" when I should stop and say, "Won't you be my neighbor?" When we got in the house, my mom could tell we were scared. She asked what was wrong, and we answered her, "Nothing. Shelley just scared us. She was kind of yelling at us." Well, that did it. In her best mother-hen voice, she insisted we repeat what Shelley had yelled at us. But we didn't really understand what she had called us. We just knew what it sounded like. So we just got these blank expressions on our faces, and I said, "Well, that's what was weird, Mom. She just kept yelling at us 'Summer ditch! You summer ditches get out of here!'"

My mother's face turned red. She literally leaped to the phone. We couldn't understand what all the excitement was about. We weren't the least bit offended. "Summer ditch," "winter ditch," what did we care? My mother understood, however, that Shelley had made a seriously offensive statement about us; and my mom was seriously offended.

Most of us respond with the same kind of indifference when the Bible announces the bad news that we're sinners. When we read in Romans 3:23, "All have sinned and fall short of the glory of God," we don't realize that God made a grave statement about us. He said that we have put ourselves in the center of a universe in which only God deserves to be at center. We have made ourselves out to be God in a world where there is only one true God. That's a serious problem!

✔ To understand the seriousness of sin, write the letters S I N in large print below. Circle the center letter–I. That sums up the problem.

You and I and every person who has ever taken a breath–even the kindest, sweetest, most religious person in the world (Mother Teresa, Gandhi, Captain Kangaroo, Mr. Rogers)–all of us were born with the mind-set "I am number one," "I am most important."

We think like this: I know God has a plan; but I've got my plan. I know God has a plan for how I use my body; but I've got my plan. I know God has a plan for our family; but I've got my plan. I know God has a plan for how I spend my money; but I've got my plan. I know God has a plan for how I treat others; but I've got my plan.

Isaiah wrote about the sin problem this way: "We all, like sheep, have gone astray, each of us has turned to his own way" (Isaiah 53:6). That is sin. Sin stains every human being, every human effort, every human relationship. Sin has caused severe problems–problems in our relationship with God, with other people, and ourselves.

WOE IS US!

To hear most people talk about God, you would think that he was not our Father in heaven but our grandfather in heaven–a kindly old gentleman who looks down on our sin and rebellion, sighing as he says, "Just look at those sinners. Tsk. Tsk. Aren't they something?" Scripture paints a different picture of God. In fact, when Isaiah caught a clear vision of God—high, holy, and lifted up—he cried out, "Woe to me! I am ruined! For I am a man of unclean lips, and I live among a people of unclean lips" (Isaiah 6:5). In that one brief moment, Isaiah got a grasp of the bad news: We humans have a problem.

✔ Read Romans 1:18–2:2 where Paul writes in detail about the human problem. (Put a check beside this instruction when you finish reading.)

WHERE THERE'S A FALL, THERE'S A CRASH

The end result of all this—rejecting God's plan and breaking God's law—is that all humans face a crash, big time. The Scripture says the consequence of our sin is death—not just the eternal death that everybody talks about. This crash is the little-by-little death we see around us and even experience in our own lives.

Bill struggled with this kind of death when he found out his parents were splitting up. A little chunk of his world had died. When Sally and her boyfriend allowed their physical relationship to go too far, she experienced this kind of death. She faced oppressive feelings of guilt and fear that she hadn't expected to feel. She knew deep down that a part of her had died.

We can't really understand that the good news is really good news until we understand that the bad news is really bad news. God has an incredible plan about how life is to be lived in relationship with him. On the other hand, we have this deep, incurable problem of sin that separates us from God's plan. And we're left with a death penalty to live out and experience on a daily basis into all eternity.

But here's the good news: God sent his Son to live on earth—a person who was fully human but also a human who was fully God. Jesus "fleshed out" for us what God is really like. He gave us a living picture of the heart and mind of God. Unlike any other human who has ever lived, Jesus lived his life with absolutely no sin. He was perfect.

It was Jesus' life that set the stage for one of the most earth-shattering, life-changing, history-making deaths in the history of human beings.

THE BEAUTIFUL FEAT

Jesus died on a lonely hilltop outside Jerusalem, at a place called Calvary. By dying a brutal, excruciating, and humiliating death, Jesus took the rap for our sin and rebellion. You see, the holy God who is the perfect judge couldn't overlook our sin. But the loving and compassionate God who is our Father didn't want to oversee our death and judgment. So, in effect, he first judged our penalty to be death, then stepped down from the judgment seat and sent his only Son, Jesus, to pay that penalty for us. That's what you call great news.

Now if Jesus had stayed in the grave after his bloody death, there wouldn't have been much to get excited about. But that's what makes that first Easter morning so incredible: Death couldn't keep Jesus down! He broke out of the tomb, and by his resurrection, declared that death itself would die.

What this beautiful feat means is that by believing in Jesus and by receiving his sacrifice on our behalf, not only can we be saved by his death, but we can also be saved by his life. In other words, Jesus didn't only die for us; he rose to live through us, to love through us, and to help us live out God's plan.

"YEAH, BUT WHAT DOES THAT HAVE TO DO WITH ME?"

That's where we come in. Actually, that's where we go out. The last words Jesus spoke to his followers were, "Therefore go and make disciples of all nations, baptizing them in the name of the Father and of the Son and of the Holy Spirit, and teaching them to obey everything I have commanded you. And surely I am with you always, to the very end of the age" (Matthew 28:19–20).

Jesus commanded us to get our beautiful feet moving, to tell the world that we need not live in a narrow little crawl space of sin where life is lonely, dark, and scary. The Father has sent his Son, Jesus, to open the door out of the darkness and into the light. Our good news announcement is that we have a choice to make. We can choose to be lost without Jesus, or we can choose to live life with Jesus.

Jesus put the choice this way: "I am the gate; whoever enters through me will be saved. He will come in and go out, and find pasture. . . . I have come that they may have life, and have it to the full. I am the good shepherd. The good shepherd lays down his life for the sheep" (John 10:9–11). Jesus didn't call us to announce to people that we are perfect, totally together, spiritual Jedi knights. He called us to announce the good news that Jesus has arrived and that there is life in him.

"BUT MY FEET AREN'T BEAUTIFUL."

If you're like most people, you probably don't see yourself sitting in study hall and casually leaning over to tell your friends about Jesus. We fear our friends won't listen to us—or worse yet, that maybe they will listen to us and think we're strange. We think, How will I know what to say? What if they ask hard questions? Won't I sound judgmental? Maybe I'm too young to talk to my friends about something this important. What if they don't think my feet are beautiful?

Good questions. Tough questions. We're going to consider some of these questions later. Right now, relax and rejoice. The message and not the messenger is what makes our feet "beautiful on the mountains." Throughout history God has called people with not-so-beautiful feet (just like you) to do great works. God doesn't need our ability; God needs our willingness.

Bilbo, the little hobbit in J.R.R. Tolkien's *Fellowship of the Ring*, expressed how we sometimes feel about announcing the good news: "I am not made for perilous quests. I wish I had never seen the Ring! Why did it come to me? Why was I chosen?" The wizard Gandalf responded, "Such questions cannot be answered. You may be sure that it was not for any merit that others do not possess: not for power or wisdom, at any rate. But you have been chosen, and you must therefore use such strength and heart and wits as you have."

Isaiah, when he was first confronted with a real sense of God's plan and God's call, knew himself to be incapable of a mission like that. He saw himself as doomed because every word that passed his lips was sinful. No matter. God reached down and touched Isaiah's lips, and Isaiah became a mouthpiece for God. Then when God said, "Whom shall I send? And who will go for us?" Isaiah stood on his beautiful feet and answered, "Here I am. Send me!"

TELLING YOUR STORY

CHAPTER 2

You can tell a lot about people just by studying their feet. Researchers from the Harvard School of Public Health did a study in the early 1980s in which they asked for the toenail clippings of 100,000 nurses. The reason for this unusual request in the name of science was to research people's day-by-day intake of an obscure trace element called selenium.

The researchers theorized that tracking the chemical path of selenium would help them uncover some significant medical mysteries. Although I don't have the latest findings of the study, I'm happy to report that Dr. Walter Willet, one of the project leaders, collected over 50,000 sets of toenail clippings. Who knows? Feet may be the key to the marvels of science!

You may not have much personal respect for your feet, but those guys take a tremendous amount of wear and tear just getting you around. In an average lifetime, your feet carry you about 115,000 miles, equal to about thirty-five trips across North America or five laps around the entire earth or a jog halfway to the moon. When you talk about feet, you are talking about movement! That's one reason the Bible describes feet as beautiful—feet help us get out and about to announce the good news.

Feet not only help us take a walk; they help us take a stand. Athletes, for instance, wear cleats on their shoes to stabilize their feet for a strong stand. A weak stand means getting pushed around by opponents, getting knocked over, or maybe slipping at the wrong moment.

In this chapter we're going to talk about what beautiful feet represent in your Christian life, that is, your willingness to go for Christ or your willingness to take a stand for Christ. In a word we're talking about your witness.

WITNESS

Whenever I hear the word *witness* I think about stark signs along the highway that say "Turn to God" or I think of old rusted-out church buses that say on the back door, "Repent." (I used to joke with my buddies that on the back of a bus like that the sign should say, "Repaint!")

Basically, to witness is to speak from firsthand experience. Witness describes what John did when he wrote:

> That which was from the beginning, which we have heard, which we have seen with our eyes, which we have looked at and our hands have touched—this we proclaim concerning the Word of life. The life appeared; we have seen it and testify to it, and we proclaim to you the eternal life, which was with the Father and has appeared to us. We proclaim to you what we have seen and heard, so that you also may have fellowship with us. And our fellowship is with the Father and with his Son, Jesus Christ. (1 John 1:1–3)

Our witnessing should say, This experience is something we know firsthand, not merely a statement of faith we once memorized in confirmation class.

✔ Reread the passage from 1 John. In the space below jot down the statements that describe John's first-hand experience of Jesus Christ.

When we witness to other people, we simply tell them what we know to be true about Jesus Christ. We aren't saying we know all the answers or that we're candidates for sainthood. We are saying that we know the Answer and that we're willing to share our findings with others. As one pastor put it, "Witnessing is simply one beggar telling another beggar where to find bread."

A lot of us can't see ourselves as witnesses. We see witnessing as knocking on doors and aggressively pressing people to "turn or burn." Others of us feel we don't know enough be witnesses–someone might ask deep theological questions that we can't answer.

But witnessing doesn't need to be that way. It doesn't necessarily involve rude, annoying encounters with unsuspecting victims nor is it fielding some deep theological questions. Witnessing is simply telling what Christ is doing in your life. And no one is better suited to share that than you are.

THREE STYLES OF WITNESSING

There are three basic approaches to witnessing: the salesman approach, the chameleon approach, and the signpost approach.

✔ ***The salesman approach*** reduces witnessing to a technique, with Jesus and the Christian faith as products to be sold. Christians using this approach come on with a big smile, give 'em the pitch, sweeten the deal as much as possible, and then push for a close. Not only does the sales approach encourage us to present an easy-to-swallow, watered-down gospel, but the salesman also often comes across as phony.

It makes me think of TV spots for "K-Tel Christianity" or "Used Car Witnessing" that accidentally on purpose leave out the less appealing parts of the gospel message. Why mention something crude like sin, for instance? Sin has no pizzazz. Sin doesn't sell. The trouble is, sin is true; and a witness is nothing if he or she is not trustworthy.

The problem with the sales approach to witnessing is that it's not real–it's about projecting an image. The sales approach makes us feel that we're not good witnesses unless we always show a hundred teeth and talk about how God has "blessed us" with a winning lottery ticket. That's about as far from New Testament witnessing as you can get.

✔ ***The chameleon approach*** allows Christian witnesses to imitate the little lizard that changes colors to blend with its background. When chameleons are at home watching television, they blend into the color of their couch. When they head out for a round of golf, they turn green to match the grass. A chameleon can change color to fit nicely into any background. (The only real problem chameleons have is when they are on a plaid background. It tends to make them throw up!)

The chameleon approach to witnessing claims that the best way to get people excited about Jesus is for Christians to act like regular people, fitting in with everybody else at school. After all, how good a witness can we be if we come off looking like some kind of religious freak?

To some extent, blending in is a good idea. We don't further the cause of Christ by being weird or obnoxious just for the sake of being different. On the other hand, consistently living the Christian life will probably make us appear different from most of the people around us. If most people are floating downstream, and we turn our boat around and start sailing upstream, some people are going to think we're just being weird. They don't know what we know, though—a few miles downstream there's a huge waterfall.

Beware of the false notion that the best way to witness for Christ is to "be a nice guy": always agree, never confront, and never cause problems. We can be so diplomatic and bland for fear of turning people off that we never turn people on. We're safe. We're harmless. In fact, we may as well not even be present! Jesus told his followers they were like salt for all mankind. "But if the salt loses its saltiness," he warned, "how can it be made salty again? It is no longer good for anything, except to be thrown out and trampled by men" (Matthew 5:13).

Effective witnesses certainly take time to earn the right to be heard and are sensitive to how others see and hear them. The old saying is true: "We need to be winsome if we hope to win some."

A witness, however, is not someone who tests the water to see what everyone is saying and doing and then says and does the same. A witness, in a caring, sensitive way, seeks to share what he or she knows to be true—even if that doesn't blend in with the background. We aren't called to stand out and be weird. We're called to take a stand and to be Christlike, even if some people think we're weird.

✔ ***The signpost approach.*** Signposts are great. Just when you think you're hopelessly lost, you catch a glimpse of that one sign on the freeway pointing out the way to go. The sign doesn't ask for thanks, doesn't get cocky, doesn't draw attention to itself. The sign just tells the truth—consistently.

That doesn't mean that signposts always bring good news. They don't. I recently spent one hour driving the wrong direction through the outskirts of Toronto until a sign gave me the bad news that I was headed the wrong way. Although this information irritated me, I didn't stop to yell at the sign. I knew the sign was telling the truth.

Our role as witnesses is to be signposts pointing people to Jesus Christ. That means we don't need pitches, gimmicks, or techniques. We simply need to tell our story about what Jesus has done in our life. To put it simply, we need to work hard to be real and to make sure that, as consistently as possible, we point to Jesus Christ as Lord. What it boils down to is a lifestyle of witnessing that gives you the freedom to be you but also challenges you to be the person Christ has called you to be.

"THIS LITTLE LIFE OF MINE, I'M GONNA LET IT SIGN"

A signpost lifestyle means we witness differently in different situations. Essentially, this lifestyle means witnessing by what we are, by what we do, and by what we say. When Jesus told his disciples that they were the salt of the earth or like a light for the whole world, he was saying that the most powerful form of witness is simply being who we are in Christ. Light doesn't have to do anything but be itself, and it will radically change the darkness. Salt doesn't have to do anything but be itself, and it will radically change the flavor of the food it touches.

Your witness at your school isn't based on your being a religious phony. Your witness for Christ is based on the fact that God has been working in you (Philippians 1:3–7). He is still at work in you (Philippians 2:13). Your most powerful witness for Jesus is being real, being honest, being who you are in Christ.

I have talked with students who have told me they don't feel they can ever let anyone know they're struggling with a problem at home or at school because that would blow their witness. Wrong! That's just what your friends need to see—that people who have real-life, everyday problems like zits on their faces, parents on their cases, and the opposite sex on their minds, are those in whom Jesus lives and does his work.

We also witness by what we do. Paul wrote the following to the church at Corinth:

> When I came to you, brothers, I did not come with eloquence or superior wisdom as I proclaimed to you the testimony about God. For I resolved to know nothing while I was with you except Jesus Christ and him crucified. *I came to you in weakness and fear and with much trembling* [emphasis mine]. My message and my preaching were not with wise and persuasive words, but with a demonstration of the Spirit's power, so that your faith might not rest on men's wisdom, but on God's power. (1 Corinthians 2:1–5)

Paul realized he witnessed to people by who he was and by what he said, but he knew that what really made people strain to hear his words was the *demonstration* of the power of God's Spirit in his life.

Everybody knows talk is cheap. A signpost witness is a witness who points to Jesus Christ by the way he or she lives on a daily basis. Saying that we believe God is love is not enough. People watch what we do, and it whets their appetite for what we say. People watch to see if we relate differently to our friends, to the school nerd, to our teachers (ouch!), or to our parents. People want to see our *demonstration* of the Spirit and power.

✔ What might high school students look like who consistently demonstrate the gospel of Jesus Christ? I'm not asking about their appearance; rather, how would what they do be different from their peers? Imagine you are one of those students. In the following space write ten positive ways that you could demonstrate that Jesus is real in your life. (Don't list those things you would not do, but those things that you would do.)

At home:

At school:

Elsewhere:

It's interesting to note that as powerful as Paul's life was in his daily demonstration of his love for Christ, his witness still involved speaking—telling how Christ had come into his life and changed him. Throughout the book of Acts, we read about Paul, willing and eager to tell the story about how he came to know Jesus Christ.

✔ Read the account in Acts 22:1–21 of how Paul met Jesus. Here he's sharing his story with a large group of people.

✔ Read Acts 26:1–29 to eavesdrop on an instance in which Paul shared this same story with a few individuals.

Paul took every opportunity to share with people the story of his confrontation with and response to the good news of Jesus. Paul had beautiful feet.

To be a signpost witness means that we are willing and able to tell in words our story about Jesus' work in our lives. Even being and doing alone are not enough. I've heard people excuse themselves from this call by saying, "I don't need to say it; I just live it." Think of it. What these folks are saying is that they're living such an incredibly holy and righteous Christlike life that they don't need to tell people they are Christians—people plainly see the glow.

Give me a break! Paul felt compelled to add his words to his deeds. Jesus even added his words to his deeds—and both of them did a fair job of living the Christian life! The fact is that no matter how well we live the Christian life, we still need to explain our actions and our thoughts by speaking out.

If we don't speak out, we won't be signposts pointing to Jesus; we'll be signposts pointing to ourselves. Or we'll just be blank signposts pointing the way—but the way to what? the way to where? That's why Paul wasn't uptight that he didn't always speak with lofty theological words and heavy philosophical arguments. He wrote, "My speech and my message were not in lofty words of wisdom ... that your faith might not rest in the wisdom, but in the power of God."

TELLING YOUR STORY

Cheryl, a high school junior, was in a lot of ways like every other student at Jessup County High School. She didn't like cafeteria food, and she struggled with trigonometry—a lot. But Cheryl had beautiful feet. She told me how she had listened to a girl at school who had been wrestling with some problems. Along with showing concern, Cheryl also told this girl the story about how Jesus was working in her own life and how he wanted very much to work in this girl's life, too. Cheryl was a signpost.

Keith was expected to give the usual "go for your dreams" speech when he stood up one hot, June evening to deliver the valedictorian speech at his commencement. What the graduates and their families heard instead was Keith's story of coming to know Jesus and how Jesus was helping Keith reshape his dreams to fit in with God's plan. Keith stood up on beautiful feet and took a stand for Jesus.

You are also called to tell your story—maybe not in front of a commencement audience, though. If you're consistently living as a signpost—being, doing, and talking about your faith—opportunities will come up at the lunch table, during study hall, on a date, at a party, in your youth group, around the family dinner table, or in the locker room. Your witness doesn't have to come through a canned sales pitch or lofty philosophical treatise. You just tell your story—how you came to understand the good news announcement that God has a plan and we have a problem, and how you chose to accept God's solution to that problem.

"BUT WHAT WOULD I SAY?"

I'm glad you asked that question. This is the fun part. Your story is totally your own. Nobody can tell it like you can. To help you think through your story, work on the following questions for a few minutes:

✔ What were some of the earliest influences in your life that got you thinking about Jesus? Was it the influence of a family member or your home life or a Sunday school teacher? Or would you trace your spiritual roots back to some friend or coach or youth minister or pastor? Jot your thoughts below.

✔ What was your life like before you met Jesus? Don't go into a lot of juicy details here. I've heard people spend lots of time telling several incidents from their lives before becoming a Christian. When a speaker like that finally gets around to talking about Jesus, I begin to wonder what her or his favorite part of the story is. Read through Paul's testimony one more time (Acts 22 and 26) to get an idea of how much you need to talk about your past. Jot your thoughts in the space below.

✔ How or when did you decide to get serious about Jesus? Perhaps you can't remember a time when you didn't feel some commitment to Christ. Can you remember a point, though, when you realized that the Christian faith was no longer just your church's faith or your parents' faith but your own faith? Record your thoughts below.

✔ What is Jesus doing in your life right now? What struggles is he helping you deal with? In what specific ways has he made himself real to you? How is he helping you reshape your thinking and your values so that you're growing to be like him? Your answers shouldn't be ancient history; they should reflect current events. Write down what's happening.

Congratulations. You have just written your story, your unique announcement of the good news. Now get those beautiful feet moving and go tell your story. Watch yourself over the next few weeks. Are you a signpost? Are you being, doing, and speaking the gospel?

Those research scientists "hit the toenail on the head," so to speak. Feet can tell a lot about your physical life. We've seen that you can also tell a lot about your spiritual health just by studying your feet—your willingness to go for Jesus, and your willingness to stand for Jesus.

I WISH I KNEW WHAT TO SAY WHEN...

CHAPTER

Have you ever been in an argument, discussion, or debate when you knew what you wanted to say but couldn't find the right words? Then as soon as everybody disappeared and you were all alone, you thought of all these incredible, profound statements that would have totally blown everyone away.

One of the reasons that is so frustrating is we feel as if we've "lost the moment" or "lost the opportunity," and we will not get another chance to convince this same group of people. It's sort of like the basketball player who shoots 100 percent in practice, and then, when the game is on the line, he misses the easy free throw.

Sometimes we feel like that when we're trying to share our faith with a friend. We head out on beautiful feet, only to stub our toe on some difficult question or uncomfortable situation. We feel we let God down, lost a friend, or made a fool of ourselves—or, in some cases, all three. In this chapter we'll talk about how we can point to Jesus without missing the heart of our friends' legitimate questions and concerns. Even a signpost with correct information is worthless if it doesn't face the direction from which the traveler journeys.

IDENTIFYING FILTERS

Why does your mom have a tough time getting you excited about cleaning up your room? It's obvious that your room needs cleaning. Clothes are scattered everywhere. The room has been condemned by the Environmental Protection Agency as a toxic dump site. And there's a cute little fungus growing on one wall. Why don't you want to clean your room? Circle one.

(a) You have your Walkman turned up, and you can't hear anything but the music—and the lyrics haven't so much as mentioned your bedroom.

(b) You don't see any need to have a clean room.

(c) You like clean rooms, but you only have so much time in your schedule—and room cleaning ranks on your priority scale somewhere below social life, sleep, school work, youth group, food, and fun (not necessarily in that order).

(d) You get angry about the way your mom asks you, and you're not about to respond to her when she makes you feel that way.

To motivate you to clean up your room, your mom must penetrate several filters. In the same way, your good news about Jesus must pass through several filters before your friends become interested in making some kind of commitment to him. They may not seem any more interested in cleaning up their hearts than you are in cleaning up your room. Your desire to share the good news of Jesus Christ with your friends is often met with polite disinterest, extended yawns, apathetic shrugs, or even statements like, "Would you quit bugging me about religion?" Somehow, you've got to break through the filters so people can hear what you have to say.

Distractions. All of us are constantly barraged by offers, options, ideas, demands, sweepstakes, and temptations. Our friends find it hard to hear us talk about Jesus because we are only one of many voices they hear.

Felt needs. Surveys show that a high percentage of American teenagers believe in God and that they value their relationship with God. If that's the case, why aren't you coming across small groups of people in the school hallway whispering excitedly about the book of Leviticus?

Most people awake each day to needs and concerns that consume their thinking—anything from last night's date to a huge new zit. Problems at school (Will extra credit bring up my D?), family struggles (Are my mom and dad going to stay together?), financial concerns (Will my dad lose his job?)—all these needs compete with your message. For some of us, the problem we awake to each day is simply waking up each day!

These unavoidable concerns and needs, even the trivial ones, often seem more pressing than genuine long-range concerns. How can a person feel distressed about his or her eternal relationship with God when there's a monster English test third period, or while waiting for a phone call that could transform Friday night?

Attitudes. Another filter influencing a person's response to a plea is the attitude or tone in which the invitation is presented. That means we need to be prepared to listen at least as much as we are prepared to speak. Listening lets us be in touch with another's felt needs and priorities. We won't give the impression we're only interested in slamming a person in the face with a Bible.

ANOTHER KIND OF FILTER

As if breaking through distractions, felt needs, and attitudes to gain the opportunity of sharing the good news were not difficult enough, there is yet one other major filter we need to think about. Suppose people do listen to us; how can we help them understand what we have to say about God and then act on that understanding?

For every 100 people that are exposed to a television commercial, only thirty actually pay attention enough to know what is being said. Fifteen of the thirty understand what they have heard, and only five can remember that message just twenty-four hours later. Just exposing our friends to the facts of the gospel doesn't mean much if we can't help them understand this information or help them consider its importance in their lives.

The hindrances from this filter are often related more to questions than to priorities. "How do I know God is real?" "If God is so hot, how come he's letting all those people in Somalia starve to death?" "If Christianity is supposed to be the answer, how come so many Christians turn out to be such hypocrites?" Although these issues may not seem big to us, we need to assume the questions are genuine, that the asker is sincerely searching for truth. We need to help seekers come up with some answers.

GETTING THROUGH THE FILTERS

To get an idea of how we can penetrate these filters, let's observe how Jesus handled some of the issues and questions that emerged when he shared the good news of God's love.

Smoke Screens. Once on his way to Galilee, Jesus met a Samaritan woman known all over town as a woman of ill-repute, not the kind of person you invite to speak for the mother-daughter banquet. The last thing she wanted to hear was that she was known and loved by a holy God.

✔ Before we go any further, read her story in John 4:5–42.

This woman must have felt uncomfortable when she realized she was face to face with a man of God. She knew that she had been married five times and that she was currently living with a man to whom she was not married. On top of that, she discovered that Jesus also knew the story. Surprised, and maybe even embarrassed, she commented, "Sir, I can see that you are a prophet."

What is exciting about this story is that even though Jesus knew the deepest, darkest secrets of this woman, he loved her anyway—he still offered her living water. But, in reading the story, one senses that the woman wasn't sure how honest she could be with Jesus. She asked what appeared to be a sincere question but was instead a smoke screen: "Are you greater than our father Jacob, who gave us the well and drank from it himself, as did also his sons and his flocks and herds?" Jesus gave the woman's question a serious answer.

Then, in verse 16, when Jesus asked her to go get her husband, she became even more coy. She used religious conversation about worship and the mountains and the Messiah to avoid getting back to the subject of her "husband" and what Jesus had to offer. It's cool to see how Jesus kept bringing the issue back into focus, and finally narrowing it down to a simple sentence: "I who speak to you am he."

We can learn some things from Jesus' ministry to this woman. To begin with, he didn't run up to her and say, "Okay, the five husbands, the adultery—what's the deal?" He first established common ground. Before offering this woman anything, Jesus asked something of her. Sometimes we come on to people as if we have no needs while they are in dire need. Jesus approached the woman humbly, open to her questions, willing to look and love beyond her past.

Even more intriguing is the way Jesus cut through this woman's questions and God-talk to get to the heart of the issue. Sometimes when we talk to friends about Jesus, they assume we want to argue about religion. They click into their religious routine to avoid the two subjects at the heart of the issue: their life—the good, the bad, and the ugly—and the claims of Jesus.

People often feel more comfortable talking about religion than looking honestly at themselves and focusing on Christ. Sharing the good news with your friends means that you lovingly and gently direct them through the smoke screen of religious talk. You can say something like, "Suppose I could answer your question, what would you do with that information?" Or "That's an interesting question. Why do you ask?" When the questions are sincere, answer them as best you can. When the questions are used not so much to find the truth as to avoid it, try to refocus the conversation.

A SERIOUS QUESTION

Nicodemus had sincere questions about who Jesus was. John chapter 3 records the conversation in which he asked Jesus if he was truly from God. He strongly suspected it; he believed that no one could perform the miracles Jesus did unless God were with him. You can't help being impressed with the sincerity of this man. He wanted to know the truth; even though he was a ruler of the Jews, he was humble enough to ask Jesus the most basic questions.

Jesus loved people like this. He was never put off by sincere questions. He didn't smirk and snap back at Nicodemus, "Well if you believe I did all the signs, then how could I not be God? C'mon, wake up and smell the coffee!" Jesus took the time to answer each of Nicodemus's questions.

Though people may use questions to avoid truth, sometimes people simply don't understand the Christian faith. They question in honest pursuit of the truth—that's good news. Sooner or later truth is going to lead them to Jesus.

If you're sharing your faith with a friend who begins asking hard questions, principle number one is to accept the questions with openness. Then do your best to lead your friend to find answers straight from the horse's mouth—the Bible. Although we can't make a nighttime visit to Jesus' room like Nicodemus did, we can direct our friend to the Scriptures—to Jesus' words about himself. That's important.

That also means we believers need to ask questions, to study the Word, and to find out for ourselves what we believe and why we believe it. In 1 Peter 3:15 we are encouraged to "always be prepared to give an answer to everyone who asks you to give the reason for the hope that you have. But do this with gentleness and respect." Note that phrase.

Gentleness and respect describe Jesus' response to Nicodemus's questions. Jesus didn't use an argumentative manner to shame Nicodemus for being ignorant. When our friends ask questions like "How can you believe that?" or "How do you know Jesus rose from the dead?" we need to assume that the questions are sincere and respond to them as such. One of the best ways to kill any chance of sharing the good news is by concentrating more on winning an argument than winning a person.

When most of us think about people asking us questions about our faith, we start getting nervous. We picture ourselves either embarrassing God or ourselves or both and being totally blown out of the water by the deep questions of brilliant atheists.

Be encouraged, though. First of all, no one is going to ask you a question that hasn't been asked before. In the twenty-three years I've been a Christian, I've heard very few new questions. In fact, Paul Little in his book *How to Give Away Your Faith* has an excellent chapter on the seven most-asked questions about the Christian faith. He identifies the seven questions and offers a clear and brief response to each one. Once you give serious thought to the standard questions, you'll find you are able to help most people. Even if you can't answer it, that doesn't mean the question is unanswerable.

Second, your inability to answer a question won't shipwreck somebody's chances of responding to Jesus. Your life is the most important proof of the Christian faith. Finally, Jesus never called us to be lawyers who could successfully argue the case for Christianity. He called us to be willing witnesses to bear testimony about what we have seen and heard God do in our lives.

GOOD NEWS THAT HEALS HURTS

One of my favorite Bible stories is Mark's account of the woman who came to Jesus because she had heard many reports about the man and deeply hoped that he might be able to heal her hurts. Mark 5:24–34 tells us that this woman suffered from a disease that caused her to have a flow of blood for twelve years and that no doctor had been able to help her. Her problem was an emotional problem as well as a physical one. What we need to notice here is that Jesus delicately and lovingly dealt first with this woman's felt need, the flow of blood. But he must have also taken the time to ask this woman some questions that would uncover some deeper hurts as well. In verse 33, after the woman's hemorrhage had been healed, Jesus probed with some simple questions. Though sketchy, Mark's account gives us a feel for this woman's conversation with Jesus after her healing.

> Then the woman, knowing what had happened to her, came and fell at his feet and, trembling with fear, told him the whole truth. He said to her, "Daughter, your faith has healed you. Go in peace and be freed from your suffering."(5:33–34)

Jesus brought good news to a hurting woman in a powerful way. She came to him in fear and trembling. She walked away in peace with a faith that made her well. How incredible that Jesus could see in this woman's pain something deeper than that flow of blood. She not only needed to be physically healed, she needed to have peace as well. Only faith in Jesus could bring her that healing.

Wendy came to me worried about her friend, Jane, who appeared to be experiencing ill health, depression, and drastic weight loss—and she seemed to be vomiting a lot. Wendy suspected that Jane was suffering from bulimia. Jane had been worried about recent problems with her boyfriend, too, and Wendy didn't know what to do to help.

Then Jane spent the night with Wendy. During the course of their conversation, Wendy asked about Jane's relationship with Steve. In Jane's explanation Wendy kept hearing hints of hurts that ran much deeper than a romantic relationship. By the early hours of the morning, Jane finally, trembling with fear, told Wendy the whole truth.

She and Steve had been sleeping together for about six months. At first it seemed wonderful. About one month ago, though, Jane discovered she was pregnant. She felt scared and ashamed and didn't know what to do. She finally decided to try to abort the child by starving it. She had been eating meals and immediately causing herself to vomit.

The two girls talked through the long night. Wendy handled it beautifully—listening quietly, occasionally asking questions, reaching out to touch Jane's hand as she cried more intensely. Together they talked through the whole thing—the unexpected pregnancy, the guilt, the fear, and the fact that God loved Jane enough to offer her forgiveness through Jesus. For Jane it was the first step back to health—of body and mind.

Sometimes sharing the good news requires us to deal with questions that are neither evasive nor theological. They are born out of real-life human hurts. The examples of Jesus and Wendy give us a sense of how we can best minister in such situations.

The first smart thing that Wendy did was nothing. She didn't immediately unload all this stuff about Jesus on Jane. She listened. She realized that Jane would have no interest in dealing with spiritual needs that she may or may not know about until she began to sense hope for those needs staring her in the face. Wendy met Jane at her point of need and helped her uncover deeper needs.

The process of listening to needy people scares us sometimes. We feel like we're trying to play amateur psychiatrist in these situations, and truthfully, it is scary. Certainly, sometimes we love a friend best by accompanying him or her to talk with a doctor, pastor, counselor, or parent who needs to be brought into the situation.

On the other hand, how many of your friends would voluntarily visit their pastor or youth minister when they have a problem? In most cases you are as close as they get to talking with someone who can offer them help. You may not feel capable, but you're a lot better than nothing!

In such a situation remembering the following four-stage process in counseling may help. This material comes from the book *Youth Ministry: Its Renewal in the Local Church*, by Larry Richards.

✔ ***Stage One: Share the problem.*** Listen and use questions to prompt your friend to share as honestly as possible the whole truth. Don't be afraid to probe, but don't play *National Enquirer* either. Learn enough to be helpful without mining for every grain of dirt. The best way to short-circuit this process is speaking up too soon: "Gee that's too bad. Well, anyway, God has a plan. Humans have a problem. Wanna pray?"

Guard your responses against phrases or expressions that might transmit messages of condemnation. The best message you can communicate is unconditional love: "You could tell me everything you've ever done, and I would still care about you and want you to drink this living water."

✔ ***Stage Two: Share similar conflicts.*** Be vulnerable enough to step out of the Super Christian costume and talk with this person as a sinner who has faced similar struggles and felt similar hurts. This doesn't mean you should be phony—"Oh, yes, what a coincidence! I think I might be pregnant too!" Wendy had never had sexual relations with her boyfriend; but she knew what it felt like to have sexual desire, to be in love, to yearn for intimacy, and to feel scared and guilty. She shared out of those feelings.

✔ ***Stage Three: Share your solutions.*** Here's your opportunity to share with your friend how Jesus is helping you in your struggles with the same kinds of issues. You don't need to come across as Mr. or Miss Together. Basically you're saying, "I struggle with the same kinds of stuff, but Jesus is helping me deal with it in a way that pleases God and brings me some peace of mind."

During this step, go beyond simply sharing the gospel. Your personal story might help your friend uncover some solutions that she or he had not thought of before. You can offer practical strategies for dealing with the situation. Giving a Christian response doesn't mean that every plan for action has to begin with the words, "Well, spiritually speaking . . ."

✔ ***Stage Four: Choose and do.*** In this final stage help your friend come to some point of decision—what next step can your friend take? This stage is sometimes the most uncomfortable for us because we feel we're being pushy. On the other hand, when my batteries are low and won't start my motor, I need someone to get pushy with me. Sometimes a jump start from a friend is just what we need to get going again.

Challenging our friends in that way can be risky. They may not understand our words of help. But conversation alone doesn't usually solve real problems. Most people need more than information; they need a plan of action. They need to make choices. Their choices may include spiritual decisions, so don't be afraid to suggest that. Above all, make sure your counsel doesn't sound like you'll quit caring about them if they don't take your advice and do what you say.

NO NEED TO GET UPTIGHT

By this stage you may be thinking, Wait a minute. I don't know enough to handle all these questions, to talk somebody through tough situations. I'm just . . . me. But that's the beauty of the whole thing–that's all you need to be. Jesus can use you to work something of value into the lives of other people. The question is, are you willing to answer a question or to heal a hurt or to deal with a concern when you're confronted by it?

God isn't looking for ability as much as availability. God can make you able. Remember what Jesus told his disciples: "When they arrest you, do not worry about what to say or how to say it. At that time you will be given what to say, for it will not be you speaking, but the Spirit of your Father speaking through you" (Matthew 10:19–20).

RESPONDING,
WAITING, AND
FAILING
CHAPTER
4

Sherry was upset. She had been so excited that things seemed to be picking up for her friend Lynne. Lately they had had many conversations about God, and life, and becoming a Christian. Sherry was a new Christian herself, and she loved to see how God worked through her witness to influence her friend.

Lynne had really opened up to Sherry, even asking her to pray for her struggles with loneliness and low self-esteem. And Lynne was just blown away that Sherry could actually pray and talk to God as if he were her own father. So one day, when Lynne asked Sherry to pray that she might find a new boyfriend, she did so without hesitating.

Maybe it was coincidence that Rod called Lynne a few weeks later, but the call sure got Lynne's attention. To Sherry it seemed as if God had really answered their prayer. She was thrilled.

Then things began to go downhill.

Lynne and Rod became inseparable. Their long hours and late nights together developed into an unhealthy relationship with far too much physical involvement. Sherry was deeply concerned. Of course, everything was wonderful for Lynne. No more loneliness. No more depression. No more emptiness. No wonder she forgot about God.

Sherry remembered the last time they had really talked–it was three weeks ago. Oh, sure, Lynne had said she missed their talks together, but added, "You don't begrudge me the kind of happiness I've found in Rod, do you?" That's what finally made Sherry angry—angry at Lynne for losing her mind over this guy and totally blocking everything else out of her life. Angry at God for providing a boyfriend who didn't seem to do anything but take her friend away from her and away from a chance to know God. Angry at herself for being dumb enough to think she might be able to help a friend come to know God.

Lynne seemed so interested, so thirsty. Now she acted as if their conversations never happened. No wonder Sherry felt depressed!

Welcome to the real world.

A lot of us have experienced similar thoughts and feelings. If you've tried—really tried—to share Jesus with your friends, you've probably known some of the fear and doubt that come with speaking out. You've probably also sensed some of the frustration of seeing those conversations seemingly go nowhere. You wonder if you're doing something wrong, if you're weird for thinking God might work in someone's life through you, or if maybe this whole Christianity business is just a waste of time.

In this chapter we'll talk about some of those feelings and questions—how to deal with them and how to learn from them.

RISKS AND EXPECTATIONS

First of all, stepping forward in witness for God is always risky. We have no guarantees. Sometimes we feel we have to respond. Sometimes we feel we must wait and see. Other times we feel we've failed.

Have you ever watched somebody reach out and touch a hot stove and then heard them yell, "Hey, that's hot!" You're thinking, "Uh, yeah, welcome to the real world." No one should be surprised that a stove would be hot. That's just the way stoves are. We learn to respect that fact.

Respecting the potential of a stove to burn us, however, doesn't mean we'll never get burned. We probably will. But we won't get burned every time we cook. We decide to be cautious, but we also decide that the risk of maybe getting burned is not going to scare us away from trying to cook up some culinary masterpiece.

Sherry risked a hot-stove experience. She got her hopes up and she took the risk of sharing her faith. And she got burned—at least that's what it felt like. Now, she's beginning to ask herself some tough questions.

We need to be realistic about the risks we take and the expectations we have when we share our faith with friends. Sometimes our friends hear us; sometimes they ignore us. Sometimes people soak up the gospel like parched ground; sometimes they respond with all the enthusiasm of a doorknob.

Sherry isn't the first person to meet frustration in trying to help a friend come to know Jesus. Although Scripture gives examples of believers who were tremendously used by God to bring the Word to others, it also records occasions when the messenger seemed to run into a stone wall. Running into a stone wall doesn't mean that your spiritual batteries are weak or that you said something wrong. People are free to say no to God; often that's exactly what they do.

The example of the apostle Paul teaching in Athens, recorded in Acts 17:16–34, demonstrates the varied responses to the gospel. Paul delivered an unbelievably powerful message. Every ear in the house tuned into his speech. It seemed like Paul had them in the palm of his hand. We expect to read that a heavenly choir hummed in the background as Paul closed his message with a challenge to repent and believe that Jesus is Lord.

But read what actually happens. Some of Paul's hearers made fun of him: "What is this babbler trying to say? Maybe he ate too many pomegranates!" You can hear them yelling, "Yeah, Paul, sure. Now, tell us about the tooth fairy." Others seemed interested, but noncommittal. They said, "Hmmm. What a concept—resurrection from the dead. We want to hear you speak about this again." Still others believed—but only a few. Some of their names are given in verse 34.

The bottom line is that Paul faithfully shared the good news. And the crowd's reaction was a mixed bag of yes's, no's, and maybe's. We will almost always be met with such a mixture of responses when we share our faith. When we understand this, it might help us feel less discouraged.

SOME SAID NO TO JESUS

After all, even Jesus got that kind of mixed response, didn't he? Matthew's gospel (19:16–22) tells the story about a wealthy young man who came to Jesus with a question: "Teacher, what good thing must I do to get eternal life?" Jesus simple response made a difficult demand: "If you want to be perfect, go, sell your possessions and give to the poor, and you will have treasure in heaven. Then come, follow me." Did the young man, overwhelmed by the presence of God, fall on the ground, worship Jesus, and promise to sell all he had? Check it out. The Scripture says that the young man went away sad, because he was very rich.

Think about this encounter. Jesus met a young man who, from all appearances, was deeply and sincerely interested in finding out about a relationship with God. We have every reason to believe that this young man was ready to do whatever was necessary to receive eternal life. Yet, even though Jesus took this person seriously, responded to his questions, and invested his concern, he hit a dead end. The Son of God himself talked with this man; yet the young man went away, apparently refusing to begin living with God. It was a disappointing response.

We don't know how Lynne's story will end. But we do know from Jesus' own words that our witness simply will not be convincing to everyone. "Enter through the narrow gate. For wide is the gate and broad is the road that leads to destruction, and many enter through it. But small is the gate and narrow the road that leads to life, and only a few find it" (Matthew 7:13–14).

Let's think about some of the reasons that this young man might have turned away from Jesus.

✔ Read through Matthew 19:16–22 one more time. In the following space jot your ideas about why the man turned away.

Here are at least three reasons the young man may have turned away from Jesus, and thereby turned away from God.

First, maybe the rich young man wasn't all that interested. What if he merely wanted to be seen talking to this important figure? What if he was probing Jesus to see if they might click for a business deal that would make him an even richer young man? His motives may have been altogether different from the way he made himself appear.

Let's bring the principle up to date. A friend might go with you to youth group or Bible study, for example. Week after week he returns, and you think, Man, this guy is really getting into this thing–it's incredible! Then you find out that the reason he's been coming to Bible study is to be with an attractive girl in your youth group. The guy's on fire all right–but not with spiritual passion!

People do have mixed motives. What appears to be an interest in spiritual things may actually be an interest in something else. You may mistake another kind of interest for spiritual interest, but that doesn't mean you're gullible or naive. You have to assume that those who ask about your faith sincerely want to know. You can't just say, "Gimme a break. You don't really care."

Second, the rich young man may have turned away because, although he was sincerely interested, he judged that the price of following Jesus was too high to pay. Selling all you have and giving the money to the poor are harsh terms by anybody's count. The young man may have decided that he didn't want eternal life as much as he wanted to hold on to his possessions. That's a common response.

Especially in today's self-oriented culture, some people simply aren't willing to pay the price. That's too bad, but that's the real world. On one occasion Jesus was talking to his disciples about the cost of a genuine commitment to God when many of them protested, "This is a hard teaching. Who can accept it?" (John 6:60–66).

Notice that Jesus didn't back off. But Jesus' clear challenge led others to back off. Verse 66 reads that "from this time many of his disciples turned back and no longer followed him." Some go away sorrowfully like the rich young man. Some go away disinterested. Some don't realize they're turning away at all. Some turn away from Jesus, not because they don't understand, but because they understand all too well and don't want to pay the price.

Third, maybe we also ought to admit that it might be a bit too early to say anything about that rich young man's response. True, on that day he turned away from Jesus. What we don't know is whether he ever changed his mind. Possibly he had second thoughts about this proposition—maybe weeks later, maybe months later. We'll never know for sure what effect his brief conversation with Jesus had in the life of this young man. When he turned away that day, it was the end of the episode in Matthew 19, but not necessarily the end of the story.

We may get discouraged by the lack of immediate results from our conversations with friends or family members. In truth, however, we don't know how God might be able to use those conversations later on. That's why our responsibility is to be faithful in sharing the good news.

When a news anchor announces that a chemical spill has occurred, he has done his job. He's not responsible for getting everybody safely out of the area. Each person must make her or his own choice about evacuation. You never know. Those who offer no response at first might completely change their minds as the fumes get stronger. Don't give up too soon. One more announcement might be all it takes to help a person decide to get moving.

CALLED TO BE A "SOW AND SOW"

Jesus told a parable of a man who went out to sow grain.

✔ Read Luke 8:5–8 and 11–15. Use the questions below to help you think about what Jesus was saying in the story.

1. The seed fell in four different places. What were they?

2. What happened to the seed that fell along the path?

3. What happened to the seed that fell on rocky ground?

4. What happened to the seed that fell among thorn bushes?

5. What happened to the seed that fell in good soil?

6. Jesus finished the parable by explaining that each one of these soils represents a different type of person who hears the gospel. What kind of person corresponds to each of the four soils?

Soil Number One:

Soil Number Two:

Soil Number Three:

Soil Number Four:

7. What lesson does this parable teach?

8. In what ways are you warned by this parable?

9. In what ways are you encouraged by this parable?

According to this parable, the seed is the same in every case. When there was no harvest, it was not due to lousy seed. The problem was due to lousy soil. The harvest that comes from our sharing of the gospel is also subject to the limitations of the "ground" on which it falls. Sometimes our friends' poor response to our witness may discourage us into wondering if our message is wrong or if we're sowing the seed in the wrong way. Jesus' parable assures us that the way a person hears the Word makes all the difference between a positive response and a negative response to the gospel.

But this parable also tells us something else very important: An individual's final response to our sharing of the good news is not always evident right away. Seeds go through early stages of growth underground, and the inexperienced gardener may assume nothing's happening. But don't be fooled. Just because we don't see the growth doesn't mean it isn't happening. Sometimes in our discouragement about someone's slow response, we act like the little boy who kept pulling the plant out of the ground to see if it had developed any roots yet. That's not usually going to help growth happen.

The sower's job is to work the soil, sow the seed, and trust God to bring the harvest. We need to follow the sower's example. Share the gospel with your friends and family members, love and care for them, then leave the rest of the miracle of growth in God's hands.

HARD HEARTS AND HARD HEADS

Have you ever been talking with someone about Jesus and just began to get the impression that they have not heard you, will not hear you, and aren't really even listening? It just seems like some people are hardened to the gospel.

The Bible gives us several examples of people, who, no matter what they went through, no matter what they heard, never seemed to respond to God. The pharaoh back in the book of Exodus is a prime example. No matter what plagues God sent on Egypt or how clearly Moses demanded that Pharaoh let God's people go, he stubbornly refused. Over and over again, the Scripture says of him, "Pharaoh's heart was hardened, and he did not obey the Lord."

That passage always used to bother me. Number one, I couldn't understand who was hardening Pharaoh's heart; and number two, if it was God, why would the Lord harden Pharaoh's heart? That didn't seem fair. And yet, in my own life I've come across people who were just like Pharaoh. They simply seem to have a hard heart.

Experience and deeper study have taught me something over the years. I've learned that God's Word is like the sun that shines on all the earth. It does not produce the same results in all the objects on which it shines. When ice sits in the sunshine, its hardness melts. When clay sits in that same sun, its hardness gets harder. The sun reveals the essence of the ice or the clay for what it is.

In sharing with people, we simply must recognize that there are some people who are going to hear the Word and their hearts are going to melt and soften. There will also be those, on the other hand, who hear the Word, and the more they hear it, the harder they get. That's sad, and it's painful, but it's the truth.

It's not up to us, however, to decide who is ice and who is clay. The image of the farmer sowing seed better explains our job—to share the Word so the light of God's Son can do the work. Even if we are the most sensitive, caring, and astute witnesses that ever lived, some of our friends and loved ones may never respond with a yes to God. The difference is in an individual's heart. Although God's Word comes to us all, we do not all receive it the same way.

It all comes down to what John wrote in Revelation: "He who has an ear, let him hear what the Spirit says" (2:7). We need to pray that people will have ears to hear. We also need to look at our life and to ask continually, "Am I doing anything that puts a block or an obstacle between this person and Jesus?" You've heard the old expression, "What you're doing speaks so loudly that I can't hear what you're saying"? We need to be careful that we faithfully share the gospel with our life and our lips. After that, the response is out of our hands.

RELAX, GOD IS AT WORK

The bottom line is that Sherry does not have to carry the responsibility for Lynne's response to God. She can relax. Her concern and burden for her friend are wonderful, and they're always appropriate. But Sherry need not badger herself with doubts and questions about why Lynne didn't maintain her interest in Bible study or about what might have happened if Sherry had only said this or that differently. Sherry was obedient. She sowed the seed. God is in charge of the rest.

The prophet Isaiah must have been encouraged by that fact. Day after day he wrote oracles that people just ignored. You know, he must have smiled at least a little as he wrote these words about God's message:

> As the rain and the snow come down from heaven, and do not return to it without watering the earth and making it bud and flourish, so that it yields seed for the sower and bread for the eater, so is my word that goes out from my mouth: It will not return to me empty, but will accomplish what I desire and achieve the purpose for which I sent it. (Isaiah 55:10–11)

LOOKING BEHIND THE WORDS

CHAPTER

Did you ever play hide-and-seek when you were little? Remember that incredible feeling of being someplace where no one could see you? Where no one would even think of looking for you? I remember hiding in our dog Phoebe's doghouse when I was four or five. I waited and watched, scrunched up in a little ball, thinking how clever I was. After about twenty minutes, I saw what looked like about fifty dogs chasing Phoebe and heading for the little doghouse. I didn't realize that Phoebe was in heat. For the next few minutes that doghouse was jumping. I yelled. I screamed. I cried. I dodged. And I just about got trampled. It was one of my most memorable hide-and-seek games. To this day, I still blush when I see young puppies.

Hopefully, your memories of playing hide-and-seek are not as vivid as mine. Maybe your scariest memory is the time you were lurking in the dark, hunkered down in your hiding place, making sounds that would scare the seeker, when all of a sudden you realized that though you had stopped making the scary noises, you were still hearing them.

Our hide-and-seek days don't end with childhood, unfortunately. Many of us play sophisticated hide-and-seek well into our adult years. Our hiding places are more subtle, but we're still out there, undercover.

Unfinished homework may kick off hide-and-seek as we sit in class, fearing the teacher will call on us and yell, "Negative one, two, three on you." The freeway is another scene for hide-and-seek, with drivers exceeding the legal limit while watching their rearview mirrors for the feared highway patrol seeking them, siren wailing and blue lights flashing.

We regularly play hide-and-seek in the ways we talk to each other and act around one another. We hide our feelings. We cloak our thoughts. We shadow some of our real hopes or fears because we don't want people to see us or know us as we really are. What if they won't like us? What if they lose respect for us? We can list a million and one reasons for hiding our feelings and concealing our thoughts. There's something scary about being known for who we really are.

✔ In the space below jot down some of the ways we hide from one another. What do we do, say, or even wear in an attempt to hide ourselves?

A WILLINGNESS TO SEEK

Loving people for Christ means that we realize that people hide and that we learn to get wise to the ways people hide. Once we "find" them we must be able to help people experience unconditional love that says, I know you just as you are, and I love you anyway. God loves each of us with unconditional love, and we are called to love others in that same way. It's the kind of love that is willing and able to listen, not just to someone's words, but to his or her heart as well. If we want to communicate that kind of unconditional love to our friends, we often have to listen before we speak. Sometimes sharing the good news must wait until we give a friend a chance to be honest with us about the bad news in her or his life.

Listening to what people's hearts are saying isn't easy. Most of our world's messages are blatant, obvious, barrages of offers, options, and input. Unconditionally loving produces listening that hears not only what people are saying but what they're not saying. Sometimes what a person doesn't say is the most important information of all.

WATCHING JESUS LISTEN

People communicate using at least three different kinds of cues: verbal–what people actually say; nonverbal–the body language of gestures or facial expressions; and silence–those words that are not said.

Jesus' ministry was marked by his ability to understand and respond to people's needs. We talk so much about Jesus the great preacher and teacher that we forget about Jesus the great listener. In conversation he had an uncanny ability to hear another person's heart. He was an expert at picking up on cues.

Let's look at three different stories in the Gospels to get a feel for how Jesus showed his love by listening.

Hearing the obvious. Matthew (8:6–13) tells about Jesus being confronted with a Roman military officer who came to him on behalf of his servant. The officer told Jesus that his servant was sick in bed at home, unable to move and suffering terribly. Jesus immediately offered to go and make him well. The officer hastily declined the offer saying, "Lord, I do not deserve to have you come under my roof. But just say the word, and my servant will be healed. For I myself am a man under authority, with soldiers under me. I tell this one, 'Go,' and he goes; and that one, 'Come,' and he comes. I say to my servant, 'Do this,' and he does it."

Jesus was absolutely blown away by this man's faith. He commented to his disciples that he had not found anyone in Israel with faith like the officer's faith. Then Jesus promised the officer that the healing would be done just as he had believed it would.

✔ Reread in your Bible Matthew 8:5–13. In the space below write what you hear the officer saying about himself through these few words.

There are a number of observations you might have made about this remarkable encounter, some obvious, some not so obvious. For example, one obvious observation is that this man respected authority. Since he was a military man, that probably shouldn't surprise us. The gist of what he said to Jesus is, "I recognize you are the supreme authority." This man had a simple but sincere faith in the power of God.

Perhaps you also observed that this officer was a man of compassion. Why else would a Roman officer risk his reputation and take his time to seek out Jesus on behalf of a sick servant? It certainly seemed to go deeper than mere concern about the possible loss of "property." A Roman officer would have had easy access to any number of slaves. Secondly, he takes the time to come to Jesus because his servant is "paralyzed and in great distress." These are not the words of a callous slave owner protecting his investment.

You can also read humility in this man's words: "I do not deserve to have you come under my roof." Perhaps we even see a sense of shame here. Maybe this centurion officer recognized the irony: Though his government declared itself the ultimate authority, he was standing before the One who was truly invested with that kind of authority.

Jesus listened carefully to all of this man's verbal cues in order to respond to the man's point of need. Now, I know most of us reading this book can sometimes go weeks without meeting a Roman military officer, but we all do come in contact with people in need. Some of them will have concerns about other people, and some of them will have concerns about their own circumstances.

The key here is to be sure you listen before you speak. In our eagerness to share our good news about Jesus we often neglect to give people adequate time to explain their hurts and concerns to us. We launch into our pitch before we show people love through the common courtesy of listening.

Hearing the language of the body. Olivia Newton-John's 1984 hit song, "Let's Get Physical," probably wouldn't fit anybody's definition of a Christian song. One line, however, caught my attention, especially because it was repeated over and over: "Let me hear your body talk, your body talk ..."

The song itself was pretty raunchy. But that one line rings true. Our body has a language all its own. It communicates. It responds to communication. It talks. Sometimes the messages are basic: "Go to the bathroom"; "Oh no, not hamburgers and fries again"; "We're sweating, aren't we? My, don't we smell bad!" The body speaks subtle messages as well. David wrote about how his sense of guilt affected his body.

> When I kept silent, my bones wasted away through my groaning all day long. For day and night your hand was heavy upon me; my strength was sapped as in the heat of summer. (Psalm 32:3–4)

David's body was talking to him.

At times when we are tuned in we can recognize a message transmitted by someone else's body. Nervous perspiration may cue you that the speaker is working up the nerve to invite you to the prom, for instance. On one occasion a high school girl from my youth group came to my house with such badly shaking hands that the soda she was trying to drink nearly jelled on the spot. Those words of body language tell us about a person before he or she makes a single statement.

Remember the story about the wealthy young man who said no to Jesus (see Chapter 4)? The rich man's story is one of several instances in which a person's body spoke loudly enough that Jesus could hear more than words. The rich young man asked Jesus what to do to receive eternal life (Mark 10:17–22). Mark wrote that Jesus looked straight at him with love.

You get the sense that Jesus read in this young man's communication something that went beyond his initial question. Perhaps Jesus saw the young man's potential; perhaps he noted the young man's openness. Maybe Jesus felt compassion because he sensed this fellow who was trying to come across as together was still so lost.

In any case Jesus responded to the man's question by telling him, "Sell everything you have and give to the poor, and you will have treasure in heaven. Then come, follow me." At that point we have a prime example of the body talking. The Scripture records that "his countenance fell, and he went away sad because he was very rich."

Noting facial expressions, keying in on body posture, and watching the way people hold their hands during a conversation—these all reveal what a person is feeling and thinking. If I'm talking to a high school student who never looks me in the eye, that tells me that despite all the spiritual talk, this student has some big trouble on the inside. Listening with love means we must listen for the language of the body.

Hearing the unspoken words. The story of Jesus meeting the woman at the well (John 4:7–26) shows that Jesus listened deeply enough to hear not only what people said but what they did not say. "I don't have a husband," she told him. "You're right," Jesus answered. "You've been married to five men, and the man you live with now isn't really your husband."

To be fair, Jesus had an advantage in all of this because he was divine. Jesus saw motives and discerned hearts in ways that we can't. Nevertheless, we can often discover a great deal by listening to what people leave out of their stories.

Have you ever said to a boyfriend or girlfriend, "I love you, and I want to date no one else but you, my little Care Bear," only to be met with silence? If you have, you know what it means to listen to unspoken words. Sometimes probing that silence with gentle questions can encourage friends to reveal the meaning of their silence.

It's perfectly appropriate to say something like, "I notice you haven't said much about such and such. Why is that?" or "Why haven't you mentioned so and so?" Sometimes people unconsciously hope we'll probe more deeply to discover information they are unwilling to volunteer up front.

LET THEM WHO HAVE EARS HEAR

We can practice the kind of listening that Jesus did if we want to. Here are some suggestions:

Practice active listening. While people speak, nod your head, ask questions, and use statements like, "Oh yes, I see." Listening is more than simply waiting for the other person to stop talking. Be involved actively in the conversation even if you aren't the one speaking.

Make good use of questions. Using different kinds of questions promotes deeper sharing.

Informational questions draw out details about the person's situation. "Have you had a tough time with that English teacher before?" "How long have you two been dating?" "So was that your father's car that you drove into the storefront?" This line of questioning brings out facts that let you be more helpful to an individual. Guard against crossing the line from questioning to cross-examination or nosing around. Your request for more information should give people the sense that you are interested in them, not interested in gossip.

Analytical questions explore feeling, meaning, and interpretation: "Why do you think your mother responded that way?" "What did you mean by that statement?" "Why do you suppose people are responding that way to you?"

Personal questions encourage friends to ponder feelings, choices, and needs they wish to express in response to a situation. A personal question might sound like this: "So, how are you going to respond to this stuff?" "Are you going to try to share your concerns with her?" "What's your next step going to be?" "Are you going to be able to just drop it like that?" "How did you feel when your father threatened not to allow you to date until you get married?"

Be sensitive to body language. The amount of meaning people read into the messages we send with our bodies is amazing. If a friend is sharing a hurt or concern and your eyes start closing, your friend may take that to be a sign of disinterest. Facial expressions, body posture, eye contact, and even the seating arrangement has an effect on your ability to draw people out of hiding to share their hurts, hopes, and dreams with you.

Be sure you are expressing acceptance. One of the reasons that people don't open up to us is they fear being condemned. Sometimes we communicate condemnation subtly. You don't have to actually step back and make a cross with your arms for someone to sense a lack of acceptance. We can express condemnation and lack of acceptance both verbally and nonverbally—the rolling of the eyes, the snort, the chuckle, the jaw dropped in disbelief, the gasp of disgust.

Don't make the mistake of thinking that acceptance equals approval. Listening quietly and without condemnation to someone's misdeeds and confessions doesn't mean you approve of what the person has done. The miracle of God's love is that God accepts us even without approving of everything we do.

Keep your mouth shut. You can find no better strategy for listening than keeping your own mouth closed. Listening isn't easy for some of us. We're content to let the other person ask questions so that we can answer. We let others share their thoughts while we recollect ours. Sometimes we treat any conversation other than ours as if it's strictly filler. That attitude is guaranteed to shut down any honest sharing.

Share your faith humbly. It's perfectly appropriate for you to share your faith in the course of a conversation with a friend who is in need. Your sharing, however, must be underlined by a spirit of humility. If we act like we already know it all, it should be no surprise that people feel they have little to say to us.

PRACTICE LISTENING

One of my favorite ways to spend a summer evening is sitting next to a campfire out along the Appalachian Trail, drinking a cup of hot chocolate and listening. I never cease to be amazed at how much I hear when I take time to listen.

I find that my ears go through three stages as I sit in the light of my fire. At first I don't hear anything but myself—humming a song or whistling (guaranteed to scare away bears), fixing the fire, or pouring a hot drink. In the second stage I stop moving, stop whistling, and consciously listen to the noises around me. Usually, when I first do that, everything seems really quiet—like when I stop making sound, there's no more sound at all. After a while, though, I move into a third stage. My ears begin to adjust. I begin to hear incredible sounds—some in the distance, some nearby. I'm amazed at how much is there for me to hear if I just train myself to listen.

Most of us habitually hear nothing but ourselves. Chattering comes naturally. We have to pledge ourselves consciously to be quiet long enough to hear other sounds around us.

When you experiment with being silent, you may feel disappointed at first—you're all ready to listen, but no one around you is ready to talk. Be patient. You'll begin to hear much—some of it spoken, some of it unspoken. Your experience, however, will begin to prove that one of the best ways you can share the gospel is by being a good listener. God needs mouthpieces. No doubt about it. But sometimes we can serve God better by just being an ear.

WHO WE ARE TO BE

Next, Paul tells us who we're to be: "children of God." That means at least two things: (1) As God's children we inherit the traits of our Father. As God works in and through us, we become more and more like him. We see as God sees. We seek to love as God loves. We begin to be of the same mind as God. We are willing and able to obey God's purpose. We know who and Whose we are. You might say we inherit "Designer genes!" (2:12–13).

(2) It also means we inherit our Father's good Name. And don't forget, this is not just the old family name like Smuckers or Ford or Reddenbacher. This is "the Name above all names" (2:9–11)! That makes a difference.

When I was a little boy, a neighborhood bully stole my bike. I was pretty steamed about it, but what could I do? This kid looked ten feet tall. I felt like David facing Goliath, Baby Smurf against the Terminator. Looking up at this guy, towering above me, I had a stroke of genius—I could probably just use my brother's bike and let this guy keep mine. I knew stealing was wrong and unjust, but who was I against this bully?

I hung around the house that day, feeling cheated, hating the injustice of it, but totally unable to make a difference. Finally, my father came home. When I told him the story, he didn't insult me or make me feel like a wimp. Instead he said, "Let's go together and talk to Spike about your bike."

I wish you could have seen the difference in my stride when I went to meet this giant in the name and

WHAT are we called to do?

HOW are we called to be?

We need to be clear about how big God's vision is for us, how big the mission is that God wants to accomplish through us. We're called to light up the night. Paul gives us the blueprint of that call—the why, who, where, what, and how of being lights in the world.

WHY WE ARE TO BE

In Philippians 2:12, Paul begins with the word *therefore*. And, of course, anytime you see the word *therefore* in the Bible, you immediately want to ask yourself, "What is it there for?" In this case, Paul is directing the believers back to what he has told them in Philippians 2:5–11, describing how Jesus lived out his life on earth as a servant. He urged that followers of Jesus should have the same mind-set—ready to serve. Paul pointed out that it was through Jesus' servanthood that God raised him up and "gave him the name that is above every name, that at the name of Jesus every knee should bow, in heaven and on earth and under the earth, and every tongue confess that Jesus Christ is Lord, to the glory of God the Father" (2:9–11).

In other words, Paul's *therefore* in verse 12 reminds his readers of two things about Jesus' lordship: Jesus was a king who was not only strong enough to rule, but strong enough to serve, and Jesus is the absolute Lord of the earth. That was Paul's way of saying that we need to take Jesus' challenge and call to us seriously.

the authority of my father. I walked up to the neighborhood bully and demanded justice. I wasn't pushy or arrogant, but I demanded that he give me back my bike. And you know what? He did! I couldn't believe it. I couldn't believe the change in his attitude or the change in mine—all because this time I confronted him in the full recognition of who my father was.

That's what Paul is reminding us in verse 15. When we go out to face the forces of darkness, we go in the full authority of God, our Father. That gives us a willingness to check injustice and wrongdoing, even though our natural inclination might be just to check out. Let's not forget who our Father is. We go out as children of God!

WHERE WE ARE TO BE

Paul goes on to tell us that we are to become children of God "without fault in a crooked and depraved generation" (v. 15). We're not children of privilege who hide out in safe houses and fortresses. We're called to head out and meet the challenges of a corrupt and sinful world. We are to live in that world.

Sometimes, our tendency is to think of Christian witnessing as shooting gospel bullets from behind the stained glass windows of the church building, hoping they land somewhere among a group of nonbelievers, who will then lay down their arms and come to the church doors in surrender. We would like to think this battle could be won without having to get our hands dirty invading the other camp.

That's not usually the way it works, however. Being a witness for Christ means living in the world. If you had a friend at school who was facing a difficult problem and you wanted to share your faith and your love with that person, you probably wouldn't do it by sending her or him a book through the mail. You would go to that friend, be with that friend, put your arm around her or him, and try to help that person work things out.

If we are going to be true to our calling, we must move on beautiful feet into a hurting, messed up world that is filled with injustice, racism, oppression, and hatred. We must proclaim to that world good news. Witnessing can't be done from a safe distance. It has to be done right in the midst of things.

We can criticize political parties, the injustices of student government, or even various international wrongs and never leave safety. But to make a real difference in the name and authority of our Father, God, we have to get involved in those institutions so that we can be agents of change for the kingdom of light.

WHAT WE ARE TO DO

In verse 15 Paul continued his description of believers by telling us what we are to do. We are to shine like stars lighting up the sky. It makes sense, doesn't it? To make any difference in a world darkened by sin and evil, you bring light into the darkness. As one missionary put it to a group of students: "It does little good to curse the darkness. We need to light a candle."

Before we talk about light, let's consider darkness. Scripture writers have always taken seriously what are described in the Bible as rulers, authorities, and cosmic powers of this dark age (Ephesians 6:12). This evil power in the world comes in all shapes and sizes. It may come in the form of racism, whether through degrading humor that makes fun of someone of different color or nationality or through a national policy that forbids black people to have rights equal to others. It can be personal evil, national evil, or even corporate evil. Always, however, the bottom line is the same–the powers of this dark age are the enemies of light.

✔ In the space below, take a minute to reflect on the darkness you can see in the world around you. Start as close as your own heart. But try to list some specific points of darkness you can see in the world around you. Jot down your thoughts below.

At first, thinking through this list of dark power that's invaded our world can be depressing. That's why Paul reminded us that Jesus has the name above all names and that before him every knee will bow (Philippians 2:9–10). Light can always overpower darkness.

Do you recall those nights when you were a little child, scared to death that a monster was under your bed? What a relief to have a nightlight lighting up the room. Light overpowers the darkness in two ways.

First, it exposes. Light shows evil for what it is. When you dress for school in the morning shadows, forgetting the pizza stain on your white shirt, it's the light of your homeroom (and all the fingers pointed at your shirt) that shows you the stain. As agents of light and witnesses for Christ, we can shine into our world, exposing stains of injustice and sin for what they are. That will not always make us popular, but it begins making a difference. William Wilberforce was a nineteenth-century Christian politician who was so influenced by his pastor's preaching against slavery that he personally worked in the British parliament to have slavery abolished. And guess what? By 1807 slavery was no longer legal in Britain. By 1833, slavery had been outlawed throughout the entire British empire. One guy committed to being the light, and the darkness was shattered all around the globe. (By the way, Wilberforce's arguments were summed up in a little book called *Practical View of the Prevailing Religious System of Professed Christians in the Higher and Middle Classes in This Country Contrasted with Real Christianity*. William was better at being a light than he was at naming books.)

Light also guides us out of a dark place. One of the ways you can light up the night is speaking up for truth. Just as a lighthouse exposes the places of danger, Christians standing for truth in the marketplace, the political arena, the school cafeteria, or even the locker room give warning to those around us moving in dangerous directions. That can mean anything from counseling a friend to signing a petition to recruiting voters to organizing a protest.

HOW WE ARE TO BE

Henri Nouwen, in his book *The Genesee Diary* (Doubleday and Company, Inc., 1976), describes an incident that occurred when he was living the life of a monk in a Trappist monastery.

> For four and a half hours I worked with Brother Theodore and Brother Benedict at the raisin washer. Theodore washed, Benedict collected the raisins, and I folded empty boxes. Suddenly Theodore stopped the machine and knocked with his fist against his head. Not knowing sign language, I said, "What's the matter?" "A stone went through," he said. I asked him, "How do you know?" He said, "I heard it." I asked, "How could you hear it between the noise of the machine and the raisins cascading through it?" "I just hear it," he said, and added, "We have to find that stone. If a lady gets it in her bread, she can break her tooth on it and we can be sued!" Pointing to the large bathtub-like container full of washed raisins, he said, "We have to push those through again until we find that stone."
>
> I couldn't believe it. Benedict hadn't been able to detect the stone while the raisins came out, but Theodore was so sure that objection was senseless. Millions of raisins went through again, and just when I had given up ever finding that stone—it seemed like looking for a needle in a haystack—something clicked. "There it is," Theodore said. "It jumped against the metal wall of the washer." Benedict looked carefully and moved his hands through the last ounce of raisins. There it was! A small purple-blue stone, just as large as a raisin. Theodore took it and gave it to me with a big smile.
>
> I was impressed, not only by Theodore's alertness, but even more by his determination to find it and take no risks. He really is a careful diagnostician. This little stone could have harmed someone—a lady or a monastery.

Nouwen's story reminds us that the work of caring for others, watching for the dangers, and being the light is serious business. People will question our intentions at times, if not our sanity; and the process of cleaning out and purifying will look impossible at other times. That's why Paul counsels the Philippians to understand how to carry out the mission: "Do everything without complaining or arguing, so that you may become blameless and pure, children of God without fault . . . as you hold out the word of life."

For us to be effective in ministry, we must have truth on the inside and truth on the outside. The truth on the inside is our own integrity. We are to be innocent and pure, people who can make a stand for Christ without having to worry about being exposed as phony. The truth on the outside is the message of life. That's another way of saying that our authority and our source of light is the Word of God in Scripture. Our only grounds for calling into question some of the social structures, political ideas, or everyday practices of the world around us is God's truth.

Too often we try to base our concepts of right and wrong on oozy, mushy gut feelings or political party loyalties or some other human standard. Paul called believers to recognize that our opinions of right and wrong are to be shaped by God and the message of life.

At times that standard makes people uncomfortable with the gospel, and maybe not too pleased with us either. But try to remember the last time you walked out of a dark movie theater into full daylight. At first the light hurt your eyes. You were used to the darkness.

Following the few moments of discomfort in your eyes, however, the adjustment was worth it. You could see more clearly.

Be warned. People will not always appreciate your introduction of light into their world, and you may experience opposition. Your only weapon for exposing the forces of darkness in the world around you is your own life (your words and actions) and God's message of life (God's words and actions). Beyond that, your voice is nothing more than another interesting idea or novel opinion—and nobody is going to go searching through the barrel of raisins just for that!

LIGHTING THE WORLD

If we stopped the chapter here, you might be fired up; but you might not be sure where to move next. On the following pages are some suggestions for ways you can take the light of the gospel into the darkness around you.

Starting at Home

The first place to let God's light shine through you is in your own home with your own family. Unfortunately, that's the hardest place for some of us to be a witness. Here are some ideas to help you break the ice.

✔ ***"Operation Underwear."*** This may sound like a funny way to be a light, but if your mom does all the laundry each week, here's a good way to give her some well-deserved affirmation. Next time you're ready to put some dirty jeans in the laundry basket, take a moment to write a short thank-you note to your mother: "Thanks, Mom, for washing these grungy jeans again," or "Dear Mom, thanks for all you do around the house. Sometimes we probably don't tell you enough, but we really appreciate all you do around here." But do this only if your mom goes through all the pockets to remove foreign objects before tossing them into the washer. Otherwise your note will end up a soggy, lumpy mush ball in your pocket. In that case, maybe you should offer to do the laundry for her! But if she does look through your pockets regularly, can't you see her face when, in the middle of the mundane task of sorting dirty clothes, she reaches in your jeans pocket, and behold—a short note of love and thanks. She might start asking for more dirty clothes.

✔ ***Serving the table.*** When I was growing up, I made it my habit never to get up from the table during a meal. To do so was to invite a chorus of requests: "Oh, while you're up, would you mind bringing some water?" "While you're up, would you bring some more napkins?" "While you're up, would you wash the car and clean the garage?" Being a witness here might be as simple as getting up from the table without being asked, nagged, or bribed and saying, "May I get anybody anything?" Without ever mentioning Jesus' name, you speak volumes with that one action. Be ready, though. Your father might say, "You can get some smelling salts. Your mother just passed out."

✔ ***Tape-delayed "graticast."*** I know a high school student who expressed his gratitude to his father by taping what he called a "graticast." On an audiocassette he recorded a fifteen-minute message to his father in which he shared some much-overdue appreciation. Then before his father left for work the next morning, the boy secretly placed the cassette in the tape deck and set it to turn on automatically when his dad started the engine. As his father backed out of the driveway on his way to work, out of nowhere he heard, "Good morning, Dad. Let's talk this morning while you drive to work."

Shining into Your Community

You could do most of these ideas on your own if you wanted, but it may be more effective if you invite friends from your school or youth group to work with you to put the vision into action.

✔ ***Windshield washing.*** Gather old rags and a bottle of window cleaner and station yourself at a stoplight. When cars stop for the light, offer to give them a free window wash–no tips, no payment accepted. One youth group that did this handed people a short note that read, "Your window has just been washed by a member of the Trinity Youth Fellowship. It is our way of saying that because of God's love in our lives, we want to try to make the world a little brighter." A lot of surprised motorists went happily on their way that day.

✔ ***Attending school board meetings.*** You can help address injustices and other important issues by attending meetings of the local school board. Most of these meetings are open to the public. When teenagers show up, their contributions, offered politely and thoughtfully, are appreciated. Being active in community affairs or student government at your local school lets you shine your light into dark corners you might not otherwise know about. Don't fall into the trap of not attending the meetings and then complaining about how badly things turn out. Complaining may generate heat, but it doesn't generate much light!

✔ ***Peer counseling.*** Most communities have set up a peer counseling program through local schools, counseling centers, or maybe even your church. Volunteer to be trained as a peer counselor. This would give you an incredible opportunity to reach out into your community, sharing God's love with people in need.

✔ ***Guerrilla theater.*** This idea may sound like a lot of monkeying around at first, but it can be a powerful way to get your message across. Put together a short dramatic sketch or pantomime that can be performed in a public area.

Before you discount this idea as too off the wall, look back through the Gospels and the book of Acts to see how often Jesus and his disciples took advantage of a healing or some other dramatic event to give people a quick look at the gospel. Guerrilla Theater doesn't have to be rude or discourteous to get people's attention. Drama draws a listening ear much sooner, in fact, than any other kind of presentation.

To the Ends of the Earth

Just because you're still a high school or junior high school student, don't think for a minute that you can't impact people who live continents away.

Opportunities for short-term mission service, work camps, and training conferences can broaden your vision and your ministry to the whole world.

✔ ***Start with geography and prayer.*** Americans are about the least internationally-minded people on the globe. Our world tends to go no further than our own borders. A recent survey of college students showed that nearly half of the students couldn't find London on a map of the world. How can we love the world if we don't know anything about it? Begin hugging the world with God's love by studying a map to learn where places are. Then find out about the needs of the people living in those places. A world Christian realizes that God loves people of all skin colors and all nationalities and takes the time to discover the world's people and to pray for them.

✔ ***Become a parent.*** Wait a minute! Don't get the wrong idea here. You can "adopt" a child through one of the many international agencies that arrange for individuals to sponsor children living in their own homeland with their own parents. Your sponsorship, usually about $21 to $25 a month, helps to pay for the child's education, food, and clothing. It provides opportunities for others to share the love of God with that little child.

✔ ***Canned goods collections.*** You can put a few more miles on this old idea and have fun doing it. Tell people in your neighborhood, church, or school that you're holding someone hostage until you collect enough canned goods to equal his or her weight. At one high school, for instance, the kidnapped principal was worth about 150 cans. All the food was sent for famine relief.

Sponsor a canned goods scavenger hunt as another way to collect food. Using a list of canned food products, each team of hunters goes from door to door requesting the products listed. The collected goods are given to an agency that feeds hungry people.

WE'RE JUST GETTING STARTED

This book doesn't have to end here. You can keep adding chapter after chapter of incredible stories of folks sharing their faith with other folks. The exciting part about all this is that as you share your faith with others, many more beautiful feet out there get ready to march, ready to move, ready to take the good news of God's light into the darkness.

If you are one of the beautiful-foot types, God will lead you and use you. You don't need to wait until you attend seminary. Remember, God goes with you. You go in God's name and by his authority, so you have no reason to fear. The time is now. The need is here. So get those feet moving for Jesus, and tell people, "Have I got news for you!"

LEADER'S GUIDE

LEADER'S GUIDE

TABLE OF CONTENTS

CHAPTER 1

BEAUTIFUL FEET

Goals

To help students

✔ identify the key elements in the gospel story.

✔ explain in their own words the good news of the gospel.

✔ think through and celebrate their response to the Christian message.

Introduction

Jesus told his followers to make disciples of people everywhere. The process of making disciples requires those who are Christians to learn ways to share their faith with others.

Biblical Background

You will be working primarily from two passages of Scripture in this lesson. In the first passage, Romans 10:9–17, the apostle Paul explained how people come to have a saving faith in Christ (v. 9). Emphasize especially verse 15: How can people witness for Christ unless they go out? "As it is written, 'How beautiful are the feet of those who bring good news!'" This short verse taken from Isaiah 52:7 ties the lesson into the theme of beautiful feet. The second passage of Scripture this lesson will highlight is 2 Corinthians 5:11–21.

The Lesson Plan

Appetizer

About two weeks before you teach this lesson, take slide photos of about ten different students in your group. Ask students to stand behind a curtain or screen that reveals only their feet then snap the picture. Make two pictures of each student—one from the ankles down and another including the student's full torso. Along with slides of the students' feet—some barefoot, some in dressy shoes, some casual—shoot slides of your pastor's feet, your dog's feet, and so on. Set up the slide tray so that the appropriate whole-body slide follows each slide of feet. As students view this short slide show of beautiful feet, ask them to guess whose feet they are seeing. After giving everyone a chance to guess the identity of the person in the first slide, show the second, full-body shot to reveal the correct answer.

Another way to open the series is to sponsor a beautiful feet contest. Group members vote for the boy and girl who have the most beautiful feet. Give a prize of "odor eaters" or some other foot-related product.

These activities kick off your reading of the unusual quote from Isaiah 52:7 in Romans 10:15: "How beautiful are the feet of those who bring good news."

Ask:

✔ Why would the apostle Paul write in the same sentence about beautiful feet and good news? Give students an opportunity to respond.

Let one of the students read in Chapter 1 the story about how one person discovered that feet can be beautiful in the crawl-space episode.

Explaining the Good News

Divide your group into teams of no more than four persons to play a kind of Pictionary in which one clue giver from each group draws pictures to prompt the rest of the group to guess the correct word. Provide each team with paper and markers, crayons, or pencils. At the start of each round, give each clue giver the same word for the teams to guess. Choose from among the following: witness, sin, gospel, salvation, conversion. At your signal the clue givers begin drawing clues (no letters or words allowed) for their teams. The first team to correctly guess the word wins. Each round a new team member gets to draw the clues.

Understanding the Gospel

Divide the group into teams of no more than three persons. Assign one or more of the terms used in the above game to each team. Team members then read 2 Corinthians 5:11–21 looking for an explanation of the assigned terms. Allow students a few minutes to research the passage, and then ask them to share their explanations with the rest of the group.

For your information, the following verses from 2 Corinthians 5:11–21 help define these key words: witness—verses 11, 19, and 20; sin—verses 15 ("no longer live for themselves") and 19; gospel—verses 15, 17, and 21; salvation—verses 14, 15, and 19; conversion—verses 15, and 17.

A Quick Look at the Gospel

Remaining in the same three-person teams, students compose a four-frame "slide show" explaining the gospel. They draw the four pictures on newsprint. Here's the hitch—each of the drawings can contain only one triangle, one circle, and two bar-shaped rectangles. Each team will show their completed pictures to the other teams, explaining the gospel as they give their presentation.

Your students' presentations should mention at least these four ideas from the student reading: God's love, God has a plan; our sin, we have a problem; God's answer to our problem in Jesus and his death; and our choice to accept or reject God's solution.

This activity gives you the chance to make sure your students are clear on the basic facts of the gospel. This information is critical. Students aren't motivated to share the good news if they don't clearly understand it. Paul listed two reasons in 2 Corinthians 5:11 and 14 for moving out on beautiful feet to announce good news: knowing the fear of the Lord (that's the problem of sin) and being moved by the love of Christ (that's the good news that God has a plan).

Once students have completed their presentations, explore with them the meaning of reconciliation. Paul used the words in 2 Corinthians 5:16–21 to describe our ministry to the world.

Ask:

✔ How is the gospel a story of reconciliation? Give students a minute or two to think about this question.

Reconciliation must occur when one party has a legitimate complaint against another party. Ordinarily, the offending party takes steps to make peace. When peace has been made, the offending party has been reconciled to the second party.

Humans, in their rebellion against God, stirred God's wrath (anger). The good news is that God–the offended party, in this case–took steps to make peace with us–the offenders. Even though we committed the crime against God, God provided us a way to make peace–not by just ignoring our sin, but by giving God's own Son, Jesus, to pay the penalty for our crime.

Celebration of the Gospel

Close this session by reminding students that our feet are beautiful, not because our feet are actually incredible, but because of the incredible feat accomplished by God through God's Son Jesus. When we share that good news with our friends, we celebrate God's goodness.

As a closing litany, ask a student to read through 2 Corinthians 5:14–21 one verse at a time. After each verse, the total group says responsively: "This is good news worth announcing!"

CHAPTER 2

TELLING YOUR STORY

Goals

To help students

✔ identify practical ways in which they can witness for Christ.

✔ think through and write their personal faith story.

Introduction

Chapter 2 brings your students in a natural progression from the basics of the Christian faith and the challenge to share it with others to an explanation of ways to share that faith. What does it mean to witness? This lesson teaches that, though witnessing is more than just talking about our faith, it certainly cannot be less than talking about our faith. We are called to share our faith story with others so that they might come to know Jesus. In Chapter 2 your students receive practical help for working through their faith story with the purpose of sharing that story with others.

Biblical Background

Two passages from Acts provide examples of Paul sharing his faith. In Acts 22:1–21 he shared in the Hebrew language his testimony of how he became a Christian. Acts 26:1–29 records Paul's experience of sharing his faith with a few individuals. The account of Paul's actual conversion, as told by Luke, is in Acts 9:1–9.

Paul was a learned man who spoke at least Hebrew and Greek. According to Acts 21:27, the critics responsible for Paul's arrest in Jerusalem were Jews from the province of Asia. Paul realized that the best way to get the attention of these opponents was to speak in their language. People are most responsive to our faith story when we speak it in terms they understand.

The Lesson Plan

Opening Warm-up

Begin this session with a game that introduces the joy and excitement of spreading the word. Seat everyone in a circle. One player begins the game by saying to the person to his or her right, "I like your feet." The person to the right then responds, "My feet?" The first person answers, "Your feet." Person number two responds, "My feet."

Person number two then repeats the process with the person seated to her or his right, with the following change: When person number three responds, "My feet?" person number two repeats the question to number one who again answers, "Your feet." Number two then affirms to number three, "Your feet." Play continues in like fashion around the circle.

While that procedure continues in one direction in the circle, the person to the left of person number one starts the game in the opposite direction by saying, "I think you're sweet." The person to his or her left responds, "I'm sweet?" The new number one says, "You're sweet." The new number two responds, "I'm sweet," and continues passing the statement around the circle as described above. The fun really begins when the statements being passing meet halfway around the circle.

Role Play

Chapter 2 discusses three approaches to witnessing–the salesperson, the chameleon, and the signpost. Divide the class members into groups of three or four persons. Assign to each small group one of the witnessing styles. Ask each group to prepare a skit that illustrates its assigned style of witnessing. Groups may keep their styles of witnessing a secret, allowing the groups who watch the skit to identify the style after each role play.

After the skits have been presented and the witnessing styles identified, ask one student to read 1 Corinthians 2:1–5.

Ask:

✔ Which one of these three styles of witnessing seems to have been typical of the apostle Paul? Drawing from material in the student book, the class members should be able to observe that Paul shows himself in this passage to be a signpost witness.

Time Lines

In the same small groups have students read Paul's faith story in Acts 22:1–21. Give each group newsprint and markers for the members to make a time line of the significant incidents that led up to Paul's conversion, drawing a symbol or picture above the time line to represent each incident.

After groups share their time line with the whole class, let students work individually to compose a time line for their own spiritual journey. Tell them to place at least five or six points on their time line, along with symbols or pictures. Using some of the questions in Chapter 2, ask them to chart especially these points: their first sense of spiritual influence; what they were like before they decided to make their faith personal; what brought them to a sense that they wished to make a personal commitment to Christ; a recent incident in which they have seen Christ at work in their lives.

Sharing Our Faith Story

After students spend a few minutes working on their personal spiritual time lines, ask individuals to explain their time lines to the others in the small group. Telling their story in this way will give students practice in sharing their faith in a natural, personal way.

Take time to ask students how they felt sharing this information with others in their group. Then ask the groups how it felt to hear various people share their faith in this way.

Close the session with a prayer thanking God for the unique ways God works in our lives. Ask students who are willing to pray aloud to give thanks for some of the relationships, moments, or incidents that now serve as milestones for them in their walk with Christ.

CHAPTER 3

I WISH I KNEW WHAT TO SAY WHEN

Goals

To help students

✔ think through some of the reasons that their friends may not readily welcome their good news about Jesus.

✔ recognize that a certain witness may be more appropriate in one instance than in another.

✔ practice sharing their faith in particular situations.

Introduction

Communication has at least three components: the sender, the message, and the receiver. You and your students have been talking about the gospel message (Chapter 1) and the gospel messenger (Chapter 2). Chapter 3 focuses on the person receiving the message. Help students understand the need to be sensitive to the varied needs of those with whom they share the good news.

In Jesus' ministry we see the Great Physician used different approaches, depending on the specific case and individual needs he faced. Nurture that kind of sensitivity in your students—it helps them be more effective witnesses. It dispels the notion that some have that witnessing is barging into every situation waving a Bible and stepping on everybody's toes. Many feel uncomfortable going out in that way—even if it is with beautiful feet!

Biblical Background

The apostle Paul marked his ministry by the words, "Preach the Word; be prepared in season and out of season; correct, rebuke and encourage—with great patience and careful instruction" (2 Timothy 4:2). Preach, correct, rebuke, encourage—these words remind us that sharing the good news can be done in many different ways. Different situations demand different approaches to our sharing.

Paul's description in 1 Thessalonians 2:5–12 of his ministry gives us a good picture of his sensitivity in ministry. Sometimes he spoke with the gentleness of a mother caring for her children (v. 7). Other times his words came with more of an edge. Like a father, he responded to some situations with encouragement, to some with exhortation (another word for counseling), and to still others with a charge (or challenge) to lead a life worthy of God (vv. 11, 12). The picture that emerges is of a person sensitive to the fact that a certain style of witness is more appropriate in one case than in another.

The Lesson Plan

Opening Exercise

Read the following case study to get students thinking about how they would share the good news with the person described in the story.

✔ ***Case study.*** *Can it be only Thursday?* Bob wondered as he doodled his study hall hour away. Getting a warning slip in English hadn't exactly been the greatest way to start out the week. Then he had to lie to his parents Tuesday night to get permission to go out with some friends. Car trouble Wednesday morning seemed to fit right in with the way his week was going. But the worst blow came this morning when his Christian girlfriend told him that she wasn't going to see him any more because she felt it was wrong for Christians to date non-Christians.

He attempted to console himself that things weren't all bad, though. Making the football team had boosted him into a more popular group at school, and the car his parents gave him seemed to be the envy of everybody (when it was running right). The party last Friday night at Marty's was a blast. The fact that he had been invited proved that he was finally being accepted by the crowd at school. Basically, things were going okay—until this week.

He watched the rain splatter against the window and then looked at the clock for the fiftieth time that morning. It seemed like study hall would never get over. The empty feeling inside made Bob feel unsure of himself—lonely, even. He pulled out his old green notebook, a frequent companion during thoughtful moments like this. He began to write down isolated thoughts as they crossed his mind.

> Rainy days
> Why don't they stop?
> Sometimes, even when the sun is shining—I'm still having a rainy day.
> Am I such a bad guy? Why does all this garbage happen to me?
> Just when it looks like I'm working my way up, the rain comes down;
> and I get washed out.
> That's it. Me and the itsy, bitsy spider!
> At least he's got the guts to start back up the spout.
> But then, the sun comes back out for spiders.
> I wonder if someday I'll just stop trying to climb.

Ask:

✔ In what sense is the gospel good news to Bob?

✔ If Bob was your friend and you happened to see his poem while sitting next to him in study hall, how could you use this moment as an opportunity to tell him about Jesus? Would you use this moment as an opportunity to witness about Jesus? Why, or why not?

Ask one of your students to read aloud 1 Thessalonians 2:5–12. Then form two groups. One group is to describe the characteristics of someone who shares like a mother taking care of her children. The second group discusses how someone might speak and respond like a father with his own children. Allow a few minutes for the teams to discuss the ideas, then ask students to report their findings.

Next, form small groups of three or four persons that will suggest ways Paul's description of his approach to different situations gives insight into how one might approach Bob as he sits in study hall. Give students a few minutes to review 1 Thessalonians 2:5–12 in the small groups, looking for suggestions for how to help Bob. Let them report their findings.

Ask:

✔ In what sense does Bob need to be encouraged, exhorted, or charged? Your main goal in this exercise is to make sure students understand that sometimes we approach someone as a mother taking care of her children; in other cases our approach is more like how a father treats his children. Certain approaches are more appropriate for certain situations.

Now divide the students into three groups. Ask each group to compose a case study in which one of the following responses is appropriate: exhortation (counseling), encouragement, charging to lead a life worthy of God (challenge). After an appropriate length of time, ask each group to share its case study. If time permits, they may role-play their case studies.

A Letter to the Study Hall Poet

Close this session by having students write a letter

to Bob (the person in the case study). Encourage them to say whatever they wish and to write in whatever style they wish. Ask some students to share their letters.

CHAPTER 4

RESPONDING, WAITING, AND FAILING

Goals

To help students

✔ think through some of the reasons their witness for Christ may not always meet with a positive response.

✔ think through some ways they might unconsciously hinder someone from coming to Jesus Christ.

✔ realize that the demands of the gospel are such that there will always be those who turn away from the chance to receive Christ—no matter how clearly and attractively we explain the gospel.

Introduction

Sharing the good news of Jesus Christ can be exhilarating as well as discouraging—exhilarating when someone listens and responds to God's call; discouraging when we have shared the gospel and were meet with disinterest, mistrust, or anger. If we are to remain faithful to the task, we have to understand the realities and the risks of our call to share the good news.

Biblical Background

The Bible portrays not only the successes but also the failures of its key figures. From the earliest chapters God spoke through various people and circumstances, calling and wooing his people to himself. Yet over and over we read how that call fell on deaf ears, hardened hearts, and stiff necks.

One of the difficult tasks of sharing our faith is remaining faithful to the task of proclamation when we are met with ferocious disinterest. We begin to blame ourselves or to blame God or maybe even to blame the gospel message. Jesus' parable of the sower (Luke 8:5–8, 11–15) taught that the real issue when there is a lack of response to the gospel is not the sower or the seed. Often the problem is in the soil, in the hearts of those who hear our message. This chapter uses the parable of the sower to help students think through the challenges and realities of sharing the gospel.

The Lesson Plan

This Game's the Pits!

Before students arrive, mark off an area in front of a bare wall with five parallel lines. Use masking tape or a water soluble marker to make the lines. The line closest to the wall should be six inches from the wall; the next line four inches from that line; the third line six inches from that line; the fourth line six inches from that one. Add a fifth parallel line about six feet from the wall.

Label the first four lines in the following way, beginning with the one closest to the wall: soil along the path, good soil, soil among the thorns, and soil and lots of rocks. Likewise, label each type of soil with a point value. Soil along the path = 0 points; good soil = 50 points; soil among the thorns = 10 points; soil and lots of rocks = 15 points. Label lines with a water soluble marker, or tape down sheets of paper with the appropriate labels.

As students arrive, invite them to play a game of seed toss. The game is played just the way it sounds. Students stand behind the line farthest from the wall and toss four seeds in the direction of the wall. The object of the game is to get the highest point total with your four seeds. Use any kind of seed you can get, the larger the better. Peach seeds are wonderful, but even watermelon seeds are not too small.

Why People Turn Away

Begin the session by asking one of your students to read the first section of Chapter 4 in the student book, describing Sherry's frustration with Lynne. Ask another student to follow by reading Matthew 19:16–22, the story of the rich young man who turned away from following Jesus. (You may choose readers from among those who have already played the game in order to give them a chance to practice reading their passages while the others are completing the game.) After the readings, simply comment that even Jesus didn't meet with 100 percent success in trying to bring people into a relationship with God.

Next, ask the students to discuss the following question with the person on their right: Why do some people decide, at least for the time being, that they do not wish to become Christians? After an appropriate length of time, ask volunteers to share their responses to the question.

Studying the Seed and the Soil

Introduce the Luke passage by stating that Jesus told his disciples that some persons will respond positively when they hear the good news and some will not. Ask the students to turn to Luke 8:5–8 and 11–15, where the parable of the sower is told.

Ask students to form small groups of two or three persons, read the parable, and characterize Lynne's response by one of the types of places the seed fell. Then ask them to characterize the rich young man by one of the types of places the seed fell. After an appropriate length of time, ask one person from each group to share the group's answers.

Next, ask students to form four groups. Assign one of the four places to each group. Ask each group to write a contemporary story that represents the place assigned to them. Lynne, for example, illustrates the soil among the thorn bushes; some may say the rocky ground.

Since this activity is the main portion of your study, take time not only to allow students to write up modern-day examples of each place the seed fell, but also to think about what happens when the seed falls into that kind of soil. Jesus' explanation of the parable (Luke 8:11–15) gives some ideas along these lines.

Obstacles

Jesus' parable of the sower taught that the type of place the seed falls makes the difference between lasting growth and no growth. The seed is always the same. That still leaves the variable of the sower, however.

Ask:

✔ What are some ways the sower could be at fault for unproductive growth? (The sower neglects to sow the seed; the sower sows the wrong kind of seed; the sower neglects to prepare the soil for sowing.)

✔ What are some ways we might actually be the reason that someone seems to be unresponsive to our message? Ask the students to discuss the question in small groups and list three or four responses.

Warned and Encouraged

Conclude the session by pointing out to the students that the parable of the sower included both a word of warning and a word of encouragement. Ask the students to reread Luke 8:5–8, 11–15 in order to discover a word of warning and a word of encouragement they need to hear. Ask those who are willing to share their responses.

The parable warns us that we can choke the word out of our lives by allowing concerns and priorities to crowd it out of the picture. On the other hand, we are encouraged that God has given us the job of sowing and cultivating. We don't determine what takes root and what doesn't. Taking root depends on soil content. Our responsibility isn't to make sure that people respond to the gospel; our responsibility is to share the gospel.

CHAPTER 5

LOOKING BEHIND THE WORDS

Goals

To help students

✔ understand that a significant part of sharing the good news with others is listening to them share their hurts, hopes, dreams, and concerns.

✔ become sensitive to some of the ways that people communicate their feelings and thoughts—sometimes verbally and sometimes nonverbally.

✔ learn the skill of listening before they speak.

Introduction

Through the years Christians have been accused of coming on like hit men when witnessing to non-Christians. We move in quickly and single-mindedly, telling people that Jesus is the answer without ever taking the time to ask what their question is.

Although "Rambo evangelism" may help us cover a lot of ground, it tends to ignore people's needs, comes across as arrogant, and communicates anything but the kind of sacrificial love that God shows us in Jesus Christ. Part of training others to share the good news of our faith is making them sensitive to ways in which careful, thoughtful listening before we share our faith can help us be more effective.

Biblical Background

The Gospels give several glimpses of Jesus and his disciples using their ears (and eyes) to listen to people before using their mouths to witness to people. These early evangelists knew that one of the best ways to share God's love was to show concern and sensitivity to the hurts, needs, requests, and questions of others. This lesson focuses on two such episodes—one from John 21:15–19 (Jesus reinstating Peter) and a second from Acts 8:26–40 (Philip's meeting with an Ethiopian official).

John wrote about the time when Jesus listened to Peter and heard more than just the words Peter spoke. Peter came to Jesus on the beach, only days after Peter's blatant betrayal and denial of Jesus just prior to Jesus' death. No doubt Peter was feeling guilty, disappointed with himself, and more than a little fearful as well.

Jesus' remarkable sensitivity to Peter is apparent in this account—even down to the setting next to a fire (compare this with John 18:15–27) and the three repetitions of the question, "Do you love me?" Jesus was remarkably in tune with Peter's feelings. It's not too hard to imagine the body language Peter must have been using. His nervousness and shame must have been obvious to anyone willing to look.

Note also that Jesus asked Peter the same question three times: "Simon, son of John, do you love me?" Jesus used questions to probe Peter's heart. Jesus didn't just point to Peter, ignoring his feelings and fears, and say, "Follow me!" He first walked through this very bitter memory of Peter's—the memory of his betrayal—and tried to help Peter know that he is forgiven and that his expression of commitment is considered genuine. After this conversation takes place, Jesus can say, "Follow me!"

The passage from Acts 8 gives us a clear picture of sensitivity in sharing the faith. Rather than just happening upon this Ethiopian official and letting him have both barrels, Philip observes what the man is reading—the Old Testament Scriptures, specifically Isaiah 53—and asks a question: "Do you understand what you are reading?" This pictures a witness sensitive enough to someone's concerns to begin at his or her point of need and to move from that point to sharing the gospel in a simple way.

The Lesson Plan

Personary Game

In another version of a type of Pictionary game, players use a combination of drama, mime, and charades to get across a concept. Before the session prepare about twenty small slips of paper, each with a specific emotion or expression written on it. Below are some suggestions of the kinds of emotions or expressions you might list:

anger

disappointment

guilt

shy—wanting to speak but not sure someone wants to listen

fear

confusion

ready to give up

"I'm interested, but tell me more."

"I'm not going to answer because I don't think you care."

"I'll answer by saying only what you want me to say."

Then write all the possible expressions on a large sheet of newsprint so that all participants can read them—this saves students from having to start guessing completely in the dark.

Divide the class members into two teams. Each team chooses a contestant to act out the emotion or expression written on the slip of paper he or she is given. Time the teams to see how fast they guess the emotion or expression their chosen representative is acting out. Limit each round to two minutes.

This game introduces the fact that we communicate a good deal of information—sometimes consciously and sometimes unconsciously—by the way we use our bodies. An important part of witnessing is watching and listening to what people say to us through their speech as well as through the rest of their body before we share our faith with them.

Two Ways of Hearing

Divide your two teams into smaller groups. Give the small groups from one team the following assignment:

> Read John 18:15–27 and John 21:9–19. Using your imagination, describe what the scene in John 21 would look like if you were making a film of it. How would Peter look? How would Jesus look? Pay special attention to what Peter might have been feeling and how that might have been evident through his body language.

Have the small groups from team two examine Acts 8:26–40 with the same kind of assignment. What would the Ethiopian official be doing? What would he look like? And so on.

Allow each small group to share its findings with the large group (unless there are more than four small groups). This sharing might be done by having the small groups compose a living statue that captures the critical moment of each meeting. Teams form their living statues by using two persons to play each character and posing them in such a way as to portray some of the feelings and thoughts that the group believes would be apparent under such circumstances.

Next, ask the groups to decide why Jesus and Philip were such effective witnesses in the circumstances they faced. Was it listening skills? Use of questions? Sensitivity? Their apparent compassion? Then, have the groups compose a short skit dramatizing the encounter they studied from the Scripture; but have the witness do everything wrong.

These skits open discussion on some of the ideas related to listening skills, body language, and use of questions mentioned in the student book. This exercise may seem silly, but it should be a fun way to help your students think about some of the critical issues you want to highlight in this chapter.

Role Play

You may also use role plays to work through some of the ideas discussed in this lesson. Compose scenarios involving everyday situations in which students are called on to listen, counsel, and help. Assign a role play to each group and tell them that not only must they discuss and then portray how one might respond to the problem presented, but they must also discuss how one might actually present the problem to another person.

After students have worked through two or three role-play situations, close this session with prayer.

CHAPTER 6

"LIGHT UP THE NIGHT!"

Goals

To help students

✔ understand in global terms their calling to witness.

✔ identify some of the systems and elements of decay in the world.

✔ identify some practical ways that teenagers can make a difference in the world around them.

✔ think of at least one practical way that they can "salt" their world.

Introduction

This final chapter helps us look beyond our immediate surroundings to consider ways that our ministries might reach into the world around us. Effective witnessing in the marketplace of the world gets our beautiful feet dirty. Nevertheless, we're called to take our message into the world and to reach out with the care and concern of God's love to light up the night.

Biblical Background

Matthew 5:13–16 records Jesus' manifesto to his disciples. His words are revolutionary, foreign to the image that some of us have of the gentle Jesus. These few verses with which Jesus begins his Sermon on the Mount may rub some people the wrong way. Jesus' point is, "It's time to put up or shut up." It's not enough to become a Christian. Jesus challenges us to be the Christians we have become.

In every paragraph in the entire three chapters of Matthew 5–7, Jesus draws some clear distinction between Christians and non-Christians. The key text of the whole sermon may be in Matthew 6:8 when Jesus says, "Do not be like them." In the short passage we are studying from Matthew 5, Jesus explains this distinction in terms of two metaphors: salt and light. In the case of both metaphors he explains what we are to become and what we are to be.

Jesus says in verse 13 what we are to become—the salt for all humankind. He follows this by telling us what we are to be—salty. Again, in verse 14 we are to become something—light for the whole world. Verses 15 and 16 tell what we are to be—visible. We are to let our light shine before people.

Our attention is particularly on the first of these two metaphors: "You are the salt of the earth. But if the salt loses its saltiness, how can it be made salty again? It is no longer good for anything, except to be thrown out and trampled by men." The content of the student book focuses on the second metaphor.

The Lesson Plan

Friendly Competition

Begin this session with a little friendly competition. Gather about forty unbreakable salt and pepper shakers. (Most churches have a large number in their kitchens.)

Ask volunteers to pair up into four teams of two. The object of the game is for one member of each pair to attempt to balance on his or her body the greatest number of salt and pepper shakers. The other member of the pair is to place as many salt and pepper shakers on the partner's body as possible. The player balancing the salt and pepper shakers must keep his or her arms straight out during the competition. As soon as a shaker falls, that team must stop.

The winning team gets a box of salt. The losing team members each get a saltine cracker.

A Healthy Respect for Salt

After using this game as an introduction to the lesson, tell your students that you will be sharing a snack together. At this point pass around the box of salt or a salt shaker. Invite each person to enjoy a grain or two. While the salt is being passed around, ask one of your students to read Matthew 5:13 aloud.

Tell the students that this is a passage in which we Christians are called to be like salt. The question is, of course, what does that mean? Divide your class members into three groups. Give each group a slip of paper on which one of the following statements is written. Each statement is a quality or common use of salt.

✔ Salt provides flavor. Salt takes that which is bland and tasteless and makes it interesting and tasteful. Salt adds spice!

✔ Salt prevents deterioration. In New Testament times, before refrigeration, salt was used to keep food from spoiling. In some parts of the world salt is still used as a preservative.

✔ Salt promotes purity. Salt is antiseptic–it cleans. While salt is used in some cases to preserve that which is good, in other cases salt is used to kill and destroy that which should not be preserved.

Each group then draws a picture on newsprint that symbolizes the quality or characteristic of salt that it has been given. Then the group discusses and prepares to share how that characteristic would be lived out in the life of a Christian. Finally, the group gives some concrete examples of being salty in the way that it has been asked to examine.

Think in advance about each of these three qualities of salt–you may need to give some of the groups ideas to get them started. (For example: Part of our call to be salt means that we Christians resist the trend to be like everybody around us. As salt we spice up our world by being uniquely who we are.) Give the groups at least fifteen minutes to work. It takes another fifteen to twenty minutes for the groups to report and discuss their findings.

Ask:

✔ What are some of the systems and situations in our culture that need to be purified?

✔ What are some of the systems and situations that need to be preserved?

✔ What are some of the forces at work in our culture and in our world that tend to make life bland and tasteless?

Salt Service

Jesus taught that believers are to be salt for all mankind, but that salt is no good if it has lost its flavor. Ask a student to read Matthew 5:13 aloud, then open up discussion about what the students think the last part of the verse means. Emphasize that it's not enough for us to become the salt of the earth if we aren't willing to be salty.

Prior to the session, buy two boxes of saltine crackers—one salted and one unsalted. At this point in the session, give each student one of each kind of cracker. Ask the students to take one bite of the salty cracker followed by one bite of the unsalted cracker. Ask if they can tell a difference.

Point out that salt always makes itself known. If we are in the world and living true to our calling as witnesses, we will, like salt, make a difference in our surroundings.

Close the session by giving students a few moments for reflection and commitment. Ask them to think about the three ways that salt makes a difference. Point to their pictures as a reminder. Allow time for reflection after asking the following questions:

✔ Which one of these three ways do you need to work at being more salty? Do you need specifically to work more on providing seasoning, preventing deterioration, or promoting purity?

✔ What is one specific way that you can practically work this out in the world around you?

Challenge students to think from a global perspective, while still being practical. Don't allow their answers to be so grandiose and spiritual that they let themselves off the hook because it cannot be done. Remind them that the only way to eat an elephant is one bite at a time.

With each one still holding a salted cracker, offer them the opportunity to make a commitment. Those desiring to be like salt for all mankind, to make a difference in their world for Jesus Christ, may share with the group their thoughts in response to the above questions for reflection. As a symbol of their desire to follow through on their commitment, they eat their salted cracker.

After students have shared, close with this prayer:

> God, we sit here in the silence of this place, unable to hear the hurts and cries of people who desperately need to be loved by you. It's not that those hurts and cries are so far away–though many are. It's just that the hurts and the injustices and the systems that squeeze us are not easily seen.
>
> Help us, God, as we sit here with the taste of salt fresh in our mouths, to be more sensitive to the forces in our world that stereotype people. Help us learn to identify the forces at work in our world that cause deterioration in our families, in our environment, in our hopefulness.

Help us, God, to take a stand, to promote purity, to be sensitive to anything that moves us away from the kind of righteousness and purity that you call all people to.

And God, help us to be reminded of the difference we can make in our world. We can make a difference in the lives of those who are far away and a difference in the lives of those who are near. Allow us, Lord, to do just that.

Help us to be all that we have become in you. Help us to be salty—to be present where we need to be, to recommit ourselves this day to provide flavor, prevent deterioration, and promote purity—first in our own lives and then in the world around us. Amen.

Meet Our Writer

David "Duffy" Robbins, chairman of the department of youth ministry at Eastern College, St. Davids, Pennsylvania, is a fourteen-year veteran of youth ministry. Duffy has served churches in Barrington, Rhode Island, and Wilmore, Kentucky, where he also served as adjunct professor of youth ministry at Asbury College and lecturer in youth ministry at Asbury Theological Seminary. Duffy's youth ministry also includes work with Young Life and the New Directions Evangelistic Association. He is a graduate of the University of North Carolina and Gordon-Conwell Theological Seminary in South Hamilton, Massachusetts. Duffy lives in suburban Philadelphia with his wife, Maggie, and two children, Erin and Katie.